Lindsay's Legacy

A Mother's Memories

Lindsay Thul & Diane Koster

DEDICATION AND ACKNOWLEDGMENTS
By Diane Koster

I dedicate this book to my granddaughter, Audrey, who has been a shining light of joy during our darkest days. May you grow up knowing the love, courage, and strength that was your Auntie Lindsay.
She loved you so much, as do I, sweet girl.
Love, Grammy

ACKNOWLEDGMENTS

To my husband, Kevin: Thank you for your love and support. You are my rock and my heart.

To my bestie, Debbie De La Cruz: Thank you for always being there when I need you. I couldn't have gotten through the past four years without your love and support.

To my friend, Denise Joehl: Thank you for being my sounding board and always showing me that you care – through Lindsay's cancer and beyond.

To the Family: Thank you for allowing me to tell this story and for loving Lindsay through the pain.

To Katie Thul: Thank you for loving me and for inspiring me to write the hardest part on Mother's Day, May 12, 2019. You made that day so special for me.

To Lindsay's Friends: Thank you for your eternal love and loyalty to Lindsay, and thank you for remembering her. #neverforget

Cover photo: Cameron Kepford

Proofreading/editing/advice: Craig & Sherri Behr DeVrieze

Contents

INTRODUCTION

By Diane Koster

Today is February 1, 2019 and it's taken me two years to even begin to pull this together. To relive a period in my life that I didn't want to relive. Ten months that I didn't want to remember in detail.

It was so scary to go back there and I had to overcome my fears in order to take this step. Overcoming her fears was something Lindsay was good at. Fear of heights, fear of failing, fear of being alone, fear of death. She overcame them all. So, if she could do it, so could I.

But this story isn't about me. It's about my brave daughter, Lindsay Marie Thul. Her story of courage needs to be told.

As an accomplished writer and English major in college, Lindsay enjoyed spinning a tale and, with some trepidation, decided to document her cancer journey through an online platform, giving family, friends, acquaintances and strangers alike updates and education about Inflammatory Breast Cancer (IBC). During the brief 10 months of her illness, her "Fight Like A Girl" page was shared by more than **18,000** people. So many who knew and loved Lindsay, and many who had never met her, read and commented on the page and/or contributed to the fund to help with her expenses. More than **$93,000** was donated by 541 generous people in 10 months, which was used by Lindsay to pay her mortgage, household bills and out of pocket medical expenses. Lindsay and our family were, and continue to be, so deeply grateful for that outpouring of support.

So, to get to the purpose of this book - I offer her posts here, as a memorial to my daughter, to remind us of her strength, her faith and her courage, and to remind us that life is a gift.

Her niece, Audrey, and generations to come must know her story and strangers must be educated about the unrelenting cancer that took her from us far too soon. But most of all, we must never forget her.

WHO'S WHO

As I write this, I'll refer to immediate family members, as does Lindsay, throughout this book. This is a brief list of those who loved her most.

Nick: my son and Lindsay's older brother

Tom: my ex-husband, Nick and Lindsay's dad

Kevin: my husband, Lindsay's step-dad

Mary: Tom's wife and Lindsay's step-mom

Tara: Nick's wife, our daughter-in-law, Lindsay's sister-in-law

Audrey Jean: Nick and Tara's daughter, my granddaughter, Lindsay's niece

Rachel: Tara's sister, Lindsay's other "sister"

Abbey: Mary's daughter, Lindsay's step-sister

Maya: Abbey's daughter

Keely: Mary's daughter, Lindsay's step-sister

Lola: Lindsay's dog, her baby. Lola is a curly haired black little Havanese/Shitzu mix that Lindsay rescued when she was just a few months old.

PART 1 - A MOTHER'S MEMORIES

My mind is full of memories of her. Happy memories of the day she was born, her childhood growing up in Bettendorf, Iowa, spending time with family and friends, participating in sports and being a funny, loving daughter, sister, granddaughter, niece, cousin and friend. Even though her dad and I didn't stay together, we were still a family and were there for each other. Through her dad's heart attacks and both of our remarriages, we were still a family and loved each other deeply. Nothing would test that more than when she was diagnosed with Inflammatory Breast Cancer (IBC).

Lindsay loved big cities and living large. When I took her into Chicago for the first time when she was still in high school, she claimed that one day she would live there! Maybe she changed that plan when she visited Kevin & I in Connecticut during her early college years, because our trip to New York City really had her excited. Her love of shopping, high-end purses, clothes and shoes kept her credit cards hot. Only the best things for Lindsay! When she bought her own home in 2015 (a very proud moment indeed!), she turned one of the 4 bedrooms into a large walk-in closet. My heart could barely take it during the days it took to go through that closet after her death.

Some anxious memories of her years at college come to mind, as well. Late night phone calls and unexpected early morning (as in 4 a.m.) visits. Lindsay liked to have fun and she really enjoyed her time at the University of Iowa in Iowa City. She was full of spirit and liked to have a few cocktails. But, along with that came many days and nights of worry and concern for her safety. I remember a few times that I imagined her in a car accident, or other incident that could take her life. I couldn't imagine losing her, or a life without her in it.

Thankfully, we all survived college and over the next 5 years, Lindsay went on to become a very successful and respected career woman and member of the Quad Cities community. She became active in Rotary, Young Professional Networks and as a mentor to other young women - not only to those she worked with, but strangers who quickly became friends. During her illness, the hospitality community rallied around her to hold a benefit which raised money that helped to pay her mounting bills and after her death, this same "community" created an award in her memory - a testament to what she meant in the industry and to those who knew her.

She really loved it when Kevin and I bought a wine store & lounge, The Grape Life in Davenport. She worked there whenever she could and enjoyed the family discount. All of our customers enjoyed getting to know Lindsay and to this day, many still talk about her with us, sharing memories and participating in the annual golf outing we started after her death.

In the years preceding her diagnosis, our family went through some major challenges and stress. Lindsay accepted that her choices caused some strife in our family for over a year. She eventually took some very difficult steps to bring our family back together. She chose her family over an abusive relationship and wanted nothing more than to have her family back, especially with the news that she was going to be an Aunt for the first time! She was making giant steps towards repairing the damage that had been done when cancer struck.

Lindsay started having concerns about her right breast in March, 2016. I remember one night she was working with me at the Grape Life. It was Friday, March 18th. She told me about the discomfort she'd been having and pulled me into the dishwasher room to show me her inflamed breast. I assured her that it was probably some infection and to see the doctor, ASAP. Unfortunately, she had recently just started a new job and her insurance didn't kick in until April 1st. I recall that she snapped a photo and sent it to her step-sister, Abbey, a medical professional, who thought she should definitely get on an antibiotic.

The following entries were taken from Lindsay's GoFundMe.org page, written during her illness, and remain mostly unedited to maintain the integrity of her writing. It seems as though she may have gone back and added to her first post as it refers to things that happen in the future. Read her postings, and if you knew her, remember her. If you never met Lindsay Thul, I hope you will get a small glimpse into the person she was. We miss her every day.

PART 2 - LINDSAY'S POSTS

Posted the day she set up the GoFundMe page

On the morning of April 18th, 2016, I received my official diagnosis of stage 3 invasive carcinoma. By October 2016, my cancer had metastasized and the diagnosis changed to stage 4. Over those 6 months, after several aggressive treatments and major surgery, the cancer outsmarted us and has spread to my bones, spine, lung, liver, pelvis, and femur. There was no doubt my biopsy showed that I had cancer initially, and it was easy for my doctor to clinically confirm that it was the most aggressive form. High-grade, triple negative, Inflammatory Breast Cancer. My right underarm's lymph node inflammation had proven that the cancer had already spread, at least in that direction. I didn't even notice a difference in my breast until about 6 weeks before I was diagnosed. At first, the obvious reaction was "infection" because I did not have a lump- my breast was just kind of red, seemed swollen, a little warm, and the tissue was firm. Classic signs of IBC (one of the rarest forms of breast cancer, only accounting for 1-3% of all cases). Doctors assumed it was an abscess that needed to be drained, or an infection that would go away with a strong dose of antibiotics. Four weeks and two different types of antibiotics later, no improvements. Something was up. I had some ultrasounds done, and eventually a core biopsy. And here I am. My family and I were told that I have one of the rarest, most aggressive forms of breast cancer there is. Zero family history, zero past health issues, zero abnormal exams previously. I'm confident that God gave me this battle because He knows I'm strong enough to overcome it. I have a strong support system and am not going to give up without a fight. I asked if this meant I could smoke pot now and I don't think my doctor thought it was funny. But really - can I? There's got to be some silver lining here, right? It's going to be a very tough battle for me. I know that I have a long and rough road ahead of me. I decided to start this page right away, not only as a way for those who have expressed interest in assisting financially to have an outlet to do so, but as a way for me to keep my friends and family updated in one central location. Thank you in advance for all of your love and support! XO

Diane: *The day Lindsay was diagnosed with breast cancer was one of the worst days of my life. I will never forget actually hearing the doctor say the words. With me, Tom and Abbey in the room, Lindsay started to cry, even though she had been telling me for days that it was cancer. She knew. But who is ever prepared to hear those words? What she asked next will haunt me as long as I live. "Am I going to die?" Of course, they would do everything they could to prevent that. Then, in true Lindsay fashion, "Am I going to lose my hair?" Probably. Then the doctor asks if we have a preference in oncologists. Why the heck would we? We've never had anyone in our family with cancer. Thankfully, he sent us to the right guy for Lindsay.*

Lindsay's Post 4-22-16

Today is Friday, April 22nd, and we are on information overload! I went in for the MRI yesterday morning. It was supposed to be really uncomfortable but I took some of my pain killers prior so it wasn't bad. Also, I had to lay face down and my boobs went into these open holes in the table. My arms went up above my head (the IV where they were shooting stuff in my veins while they took pics was in my hand). Ok... I haven't been able to lay on my stomach for almost 2 months. I've slept on my stomach for the past 28 years so these past few weeks, sleeping comfortably has not been a thing. I fell asleep in the MRI!! I was so pleased to be laying in that position! For anyone who has experienced an MRI, you know that falling asleep is NOT normal!! So anyway, it wasn't that bad. Got the results back this AM. The cancer had not spread to my other breast, which was still a concern even though there had not been any signs of that happening. It had certainly taken over all 4 sections on the right breast, and the lymph nodes, as we had determined clinically.

We met with the oncologist at 11:45 AM. He went over the results of the receptors. The hormonal receptors came back as negative. There is a HER2 receptor that came back as a 1+... Which is technically in the negative. Due

7

to my age and the difference in my chemotherapy treatment due to whether or not that receptor is truly negative, they are sending it for a fish test (fancy way of saying they're double checking it one more time to be sure). We have confirmed that the type of cancer is Inflammatory Breast Cancer. We have also confirmed that we need to move as quickly as possible with the treatment. They will be inserting a port into one of the tubes that goes into my heart (Google it), a little machine that I can get the chemotherapy through so they don't have to keep nabbing my veins. Before they can do that, they will do a heart test to check the strength of that heart (considering our family history- fingers crossed we are all good here). This will happen Monday afternoon at Trinity. It is called a MUGA scan.

On Tuesday, I will undergo surgery to have the port placed. This will also happen at Trinity with Dr. B at the knife and my favorite step-sister Abbey sealing me up. I told her she can suck some extra fat out whenever she is slicing me open, but I have not received confirmation. I am so blessed to have a team of doctors and nurses that I feel comfortable with and I know that they all truly want what's best for me. With me being a control freak and all of this happening VERY quickly, I'm not able to analyze and make decisions like I normally would and it's not like me to be so trusting of others but I have no choice and it actually feels really good. I'm confident in everything we've done at this point. Once they've sewn me up Tuesday, I will rest and then Wednesday morning I will head in to get my first dose of chemotherapy pumped through my newly placed port. On Thursday I will have a PET scan to see if the cancer has spread to any other parts of the body.

The doctors felt it was more important to start the chemo ASAP and "alter the recipe" as we go if anything else comes up with the receptor and pet scan tests. The tumor is growing and the cancer is spreading so quickly that it is the best option- we (my parents and I) agree. Treatments will be given every two weeks. Again, this may change as we go depending on how my body reacts, etc. I was also given the unfortunate news that I would not have the time to speak with a fertility specialist before starting the treatments next week- which is what women my age would typically do before starting chemotherapy, assuming they would want to have children one day. It is not worth the risk of pushing the treatment back to try and freeze my eggs. When my treatments start next week, my ovulation process will shut off.

As many of you know, if it were up to me, I would have had a baby yesterday. Having kids is something that is a huge part of who I was and being a mom was one of my biggest life goals. I'd say this information has by far been the hardest for me to accept at this point. But I know that God has a plan for me and I will not give up hope. I will try to update on here as much as I can. At this point I am in a lot of pain. When I'm not at work I'm asleep. If I do not respond to your messages, please know that I truly appreciate you and it is not intentional. Thank you for your prayers and positive thoughts.

Diane: *Spending as much time with Lindsay was my #1 priority at this point. Getting her to appointments and then giving her space that she needed to reflect on what was happening to her, dealing with her then-employer and trying to stay positive. Hearing that she may never have children really hit her hard. But she knew she needed to do whatever it took to try and survive. Lindsay was quick to research the disease and was constantly on the internet reading about everything related to IBC. Unfortunately, that led to discovering it is a very fatal disease and she was determined to be the exception to the rule. After she was referred to Dr. C as her oncologist, Lindsay was ready to start the fight! They connected immediately and were always able to talk open and honestly about the cancer. She really appreciated that.*

Lindsay's Post 4-25-16
Today is Monday, April 25th. I want to start by mentioning that when I post an update, I don't have the option to edit, so no, I'm not THAT hopped up on pain meds (several errors in last post- probably more to come in this one)- My Type A personality is pissed about it (just so we are all on the same page here).

Secondly, I'm trying to thank everyone individually who has sent me gifts, messages, etc. and if I've missed you, I'm so sorry. I think I've gotten to everyone... At least I hope so. Words cannot express how thankful my family and I are for the influx of support we have received over the past few days. I can say "thank you" a million times but none of you will ever know how much it actually means to me. This whole cancer thing can really get a girl down in the dumps and it's because of all my family and friends (and kind human beings that I don't even know) who are helping me get through my days- thank you.

Also, I have the best family ever. Saturday my dad and Mary came and checked out my yard. I wasn't aware that those yellow and purple flowers in the grass are actually weeds. I thought they were pretty. They are going to get me together on the landscaping front. Sunday my brother and Kevin spent like their whole day putting together my patio furniture. While my mom cleaned my house. I may or may not have been wearing my "slay" SnapBack sipping a mimosa, listing to hip hop bball Pandora and "delegating". No, I only did that for a second... I helped. And Tara brought my niece over. It was a great weekend and my family is serious THE BEST. We have had our ups and downs, but none of that matters anymore. I am so blessed. I have so much to fight for. Leaving all of these amazing people behind isn't an option for me. I don't care about losing my hair (all of it - everywhere), the surgeries, the pain, not having boobs eventually... All of these things that make up my physical physique. I'm not scared. All I care about at this point is sticking around to be with these people that love me. They're going to love me no matter what I look like. They give me life.

My MUGA scan ended up getting pushed forward by about 2 hours today. Me - that control freak thing again - couldn't deal with my whole schedule getting thrown off like that. But I roll into Trinity and get the third parking spot in the first row that I turned down. Anyone who's been to a hospital during normal business hours knows this is not normal. So, I felt good about that. Strolled in like a boss. First, they pumped some tin into my veins, then they pushed through some radioactive juices. I had to go into a big machine (looked similar to the MRI machine) and they took pictures of my left ventricle and heart. He's strong as an ox! I asked to see the pics and video after- pretty cool.

When I got back to the office this afternoon (yes, I'm working this week and will continue to work as much as I can....don't judge) I had the opportunity to have an awesome conversation with someone who had gone through the same type of cancer a couple years ago. She gave me lots of awesome information and it was very helpful. And more importantly, she gave me hope. One thing she mentioned that I hadn't thought about is that I would need to cut off my hair ASAP because I cannot donate the hair once I've started chemo. I've been growing my hair out forever... it was super long. Since I have my port surgery tomorrow and chemo Wednesday, I had to get it chopped today. So, I roll into cost cutters and they snip off about 11 inches on the spot. Like I was in and out in 10 min. My hair will begin falling out about 1-2 weeks after my first treatment so I do plan on shaving my head within the next week or so, as soon as I notice it starting to come out. I figured hey why not get the 11 inches chopped today, have the opportunity to donate it, and just live with short hair for a week or so until it's all gone anyway. I wasn't expecting to start crying as I sat in a cost cutters chair with someone who I didn't know the second she asked if I wanted layers. $13 later, I'm shoulder length. It wasn't that I was crying because of my hair being cut off, I think it was because in that moment It was really starting to get real. On the bright side, more positive notes and awesome jewels from my besties came today... Plus a blanket that my aunt's mother hand made for me. Positive vibes only!!

Tomorrow we go into surgery and I am praying for minimal pain and a quick recovery. I'm getting anxious about my first chemo treatment Wednesday, too. My doctor said that all of the pain I'm having should start to go away right after my first treatment so that is definitely something I'm looking forward to. Love you all!

Diane: *Reaching out to Terry Arnold at the IBC Network Foundation and talking to IBC survivor, and dear friend of mine, Shari Baker was very helpful to Lindsay. She learned a lot and discovered a renewed sense of hope, igniting her desire to fight this awful cancer. Shari took time to meet with Lindsay and talk to her about a lot of stuff. She was so relieved to talk to someone who has survived, albeit with subsequent cancer diagnoses. Shari was there for Lindsay whenever she had concerns, as was Terry Arnold. They were both there for her, day or night.*

Lindsay's Post 4-29-16

Today is Friday, April 29th. The past couple of days have been very difficult for me. I had intended on going back to work yesterday afternoon but ended up having to go back to the doctor's office in the afternoon to get another shot called Neulasta. It's supposed to help with the nausea and other side effects from the chemotherapy. Although it brings on more side effects of its own... Including bone marrow targeting so all my bones feel sore. Tuesday, I got the port in and that surgery went well, but I'm in a lot of pain now in that area on the left side of my chest. It doesn't help that the sternum is like the biggest bone in my body and is right there next to my port surgery area. FML!! Hoping tomorrow will be a better day.

Wednesday my first chemo treatment itself was fine but I felt like shit immediately afterwards. I get this one drug they call "red devil" and it makes your pee red which is weird. This is the stupid drug that makes my hair fall out. That damn devil. Yesterday morning I had to get my full body PET scan which pumped more radioactive stuff through me, followed by me laying in another MRI type spaceship looking thing. Seems to be a regular occurrence.

I had a bad night last night- sleeping a lot but feeling sick and uncomfortable whenever I'm not asleep. Today I'm back in the doctor's office getting some fluids pumped in - hopefully this will help. Pissed I'm not at work today. I know that's something I need to stop worrying about. Oh, and I asked my oncologist about the pot again - still no luck. Guess pain killers will have to do for now. My dad will join us here shortly and we will get the results of both the fish test that I mentioned Monday, and the images from yesterday's PET scan. Fingers crossed we receive positive information. Thank you everyone for all your kind words. I know there are several of you who I have not responded to or thanked personally yet. These last couple days have kicked my ass. BUT I'm still smiling :) love you

Diane: *Learning about how aggressive IBC is, we knew we had to try to hit it hard, with everything they had. It was really hard on Lindsay, physically and emotionally. I know she was dealing with some depression now, but she always kept a smile on her face and was always upbeat in her posts.*

12

Dr. C and his staff immediately made Lindsay feel comfortable as she started chemo right away. The nurses were awesome and she claimed her special chemo chair in a room with a T.V. She also connected with some of the other "regulars", like Jane who took a special liking to Lindsay. They always enjoyed seeing each other.

Lindsay's Post 4/30/16

Just a quick recap to yesterday's post: we ended up finding out from the PET scan that there was a little bit of extension from the cancer but it is all in "the same neighborhood" as doc likes to say. We knew it had taken over the right breast in every way possible and that it had spread into the lymph nodes under my arm. The PET confirmed that the cancer had spread north to the supraclavicular lymph nodes (found just above the clavicle or collarbone, toward the hollow of the neck). Again, this is good news because we didn't see it in the liver, lungs, or any other large organs outside of where we already suspected. We also found out that the fish For the HER2nu receptor was negative. We thought this was a positive thing but doctor explained that having triple negative receptors can sometimes make the treatment process a bit more complicated. So, there you have it. Triple Negative inflammatory breast cancer. I feel like next time I go to a party and see those "hi my name is" stickers I should put "triple negative inflammatory breast cancer".

Tonight, my cousin Emily, who was on the most recent America Idol season, will be singing at The Grape Life in Davenport. My mom got some super cute little wrist bands for anyone who donates to my medical fund at tonight's event! If you've donated on this page, you're more than welcome to come get one as well! I am feeling okay this morning but it's hard to say how long that will last. I will try to make an appearance at some point tonight- probably right around 8 when it starts. I hope to see you there.

Tomorrow I'm having a head shaving party (not technically shaving it - just buzzing it) with a few of my close friends and family at my house. I will try to post tomorrow night with a photo of my new do. Thank you everyone for being so kind- it means the world to me. #keeponslayin

Diane: More memories, the day she had her head shaving party. Of course, it had to be a party! At her house, in her kitchen, complete with mimosas, snacks, make-up and a photo shoot by Cameron Kepford and Ramiro Corrales, Lindsay's dear friends and owners of Haus of Heir in Davenport. We will all treasure the video and photos forever.

Lindsay's Post 5/02/16

Today is Monday, May 2nd. I went back to work today after being off for 3 days last week. As I mentioned in one of my last posts, I was not feeling so hot after treatment number one. Friday when I went in to get fluid IVs, the doctors gave me a special pill called Dex (something that put in the Neulasta Shot I believe- helps with side effects). I was instructed to take two of these Saturday, in addition to the other medications for side effects that I already had. Pill overload. I experienced some adverse effects almost immediately after taking the second dose Saturday afternoon. My vision became extremely blurry. I showed up to the grape life for my fundraiser at about 6:30. By 6:45 my mom was driving me back home. I laid down for a couple hours and around 9 PM it was important to me to be at the fundraiser, not only to see my family and support my cousin who was singing, but also to make sure everyone who was there to support me knew how much it meant to me. I couldn't really see anyone (I Ubered- did not drive!) when I arrived but sight wasn't important at that point. All of the hugs and voices were what I took in and it was worth it.

Yesterday afternoon I had my head buzzing party. I didn't get as upset as I had expected. In fact, it was liberating. That's what I've enjoyed most about my diagnosis... I'm starting to understand the Big Guy's plan behind all of this. It's easy for us to get caught up in material things; looks, success, objects... things that don't matter. I'm not upset about being bald and I don't think I look ugly. I look like a boy but not necessarily ugly. My face is still intact. Maybe to someone else I look ugly. Maybe to a lot of people it's not comfortable to look at a woman without hair... That's not a feminine thing and it's not natural to most. I am so thankful to be alive right now that my hair, my feminism, my "beauty"... It isn't important. Losing my hair was step one of losing my femininity. Next will be when I receive my mastectomy and I lose my breast(s). I will rock the shit out of an LBD with press on lashes and fake boob pads with a wig on. Trust. All of these things can be made up for. The things that can't be made up for... your family, friends, your health, nature, your senses, all the things we take for granted everyday... If I lost these things, that's when I think I would have a negative outlook. Until then, still smiling, still slaying.

Today I had to get an implant (no pun intended) - called Zoladex. My doctor knew how upset I was when we had the whole fertility convo... And he reached out to some doctors at the University of Iowa to see if there was anything else we could do to potentially save, or at least increase, my ability to reproduce. The implant that they gave me today was a result of this. It is a hormone therapy. They put it in my belly. It is supposed to increase hormone levels and chemical substances that are naturally produced in our bodies. There's something to do with receptors and trying to basically trick my ovaries into thinking they're not getting hit with the chemo. For now, it puts me into menopause. My body will believe that I don't have eggs, and hopefully the chemo will leave them alone. At least that's what I understood from it all. The most important thing is that this will increase my chances of potentially being able to reproduce from 20% to 50%. So, for that, I'm happy today.

Left work early- the hot flashes started almost immediately after the implementation. Going to get some rest this evening. Another busy day ahead of me tomorrow at work- but no more doctors' appointments scheduled until next week as of now. XOXO love you

Diane: *Lindsay was really looking forward to Emily's performance at the Grape Life, and she got all gussied up and drove herself to GL early, even though she wasn't feeling quite right. She had me drive her back home before anyone else arrived. She just wasn't up for it. She was so upset since she knew many of her family and friends were coming out. We were all surprised to see her walk in later in the evening, dressed down, but still having blurred vision. She was feeling better and just couldn't miss this night! She will tell you more about that night in her next post.*

It was so important to her that the Doc was attempting to save her fertility, even though her entire future was a question. At this point, she truly believed, as we

all did, that she would be cured one day. That state of mind didn't change for a while. One more thing to add to her discomfort, though. Menopause, hot flashes, trouble sleeping, etc... One thing after another!

Lindsay's Post 5-05-16

Today is Thursday, May 5th. Cinco de mayo! I feel like in my past life I was of Mexican descent therefore I will be having a taco or two today. Right now though I can't stomach the thought. I'm not sure if it's the implant or if it's the chemotherapy, but yesterday wasn't the greatest day and this morning I woke up not feeling well at all. I'm bummed- I had plans to see my friend Beth later this afternoon and Deanna this evening and have cancelled. I was hoping this whole week would be free of any issues but I suppose it was just wishful thinking. I received some essential oils from a friend of mine. It seems like the ginger oil helped my nausea after applying it last night. I also had one called "sleepy time". I slept through the night last night and that's the first time that has happened in weeks. The only thing I had done differently was apply the oils, so I'm confident they had something to do with it! Thank you, Sara. (If anyone else has natural remedies for chemotherapy side effects or just for pain/relaxation in general, please share!)

Last night my parents and I went to Gilda's Club and signed up for membership. I had never been there before. Really cute little building they have on the river. Yesterday when I got to work, I stared outside at the river and the green grass and flowers. I plan on spending more time, and purposely going the worst route possible to work (over I 74) just to take in the beauty in river drive. It's amazing. So many things that I never paid attention to before are important to me now. Anyway- Because I wasn't feeling well, we decided not to stay for the counseling sessions that they offer although I do plan on joining those groups soon. When we were there the lady in charge told me about this App to connect cancer patients called Instapeer. I'm not kidding you- it's like match.com for people with cancer (minus the dating part). You fill out your profile and your preferences and they match you up with other people who are your age and in your area that are either survivors or are going through it. Per usual- I didn't have a match. Story of my life. So that was shitty and the app probably will be irrelevant for

16

me BUT I got a kick out of it. Like hey thanks for the reminder that nobody else around me in my demographic is going through this. And/or thanks for reminding me that I set my preferences with too high of restrictions to find a match. I'm sure if I would have put a higher age range or not my specific type of breast cancer, I would have found someone to connect with... But no, just like match.com I'm not going to change my preferences just to find someone to partner with!! Oh well. I was so glad to see my dad. I had not seen him in a few days.

My pain started yesterday afternoon. I was just fine all morning and into lunchtime! I had shooting pains going from my skull to my tailbone down my spine. This is on top of the ongoing headache that I have now almost become accustomed to. The bone and joint pains seem to increase every day. I'm not able to control a lot of twitches and things that come on randomly. I've become immune to my pain killers already, plus they were causing some issues for my tummy so those aren't really a savior for me anymore. Tried having a couple cocktails the other night and had a glass of wine last night, too. I don't know if the alcohol added to the nausea but what I do know is that it didn't help. Guess it's back to toughing this thing out the hard way! I was hoping I would be home free without any needles in me these past couple days... Wrong. I'm not used to being wrong! I'm learning that the drugs and things that used to give me relaxation like a glass of wine aren't going to cut it. I'm prepared to wake up every morning knowing that it's going to take all I've got just to get through the day... So that's what I'm doing. Do I want to stay in bed this morning, soak in the tub and not move? Yes. But off to work I go ... It only takes me about 30 min to get ready which is awesome. Having no hair for a girl is pretty sweet. I'm convinced I will continue to wear the wigs once my hair grows back some day- they're so convenient! I hope everyone has a great day. It's beautiful outside. Make sure to take note of the beauty on your way to work today... Zipper merge and all. Life is good. XOXOXO

Diane: *As the days went by, and Lindsay faced new challenges every day, I continued to be amazed by her courage and positivity. She was having few, if any, normal days anymore, but she continued to look for something to smile about. Everyone seemed to get a kick out of reading her posts and she really*

17

looked forward to writing as often as she could. I noticed that when she wasn't sleeping, which wasn't much, she still needed to be busy doing something (watching TV, games on her phone, work on her computer, etc...) and continued to look to the future and make plans. Whether it was just planning her week, or planning to take a trip when she was "feeling better".

Lindsay's Post 5-9-16

Today is Monday, May 9th. I have not posted in a few days because I had been feeling really good - no news is good news. I got through Thursday, didn't end up getting enough of an appetite to enjoy that taco though - boo! Friday and Saturday were great. I worked almost a full day Friday and spent Saturday enjoying the beautiful weather in my yard. Was able to spend the morning chatting with Deanna, my mentor and one of my best friends. About 5 PM I went to the grape life to sit with Jackie while she held her pick-up of the #slaysquad shirts and glasses that people purchased. My other friend Kristin came to sit with us, too. Thank you so much to everyone that participated- we hope you love your items!

I am so thankful for my friend Jacqueline. She has been one of the greatest friends I've ever had and I'm so glad to have her in my life... Along with so many of you who are reading this. It bothers me that I can't put out appreciation press releases to tell the world how thankful I am. I hope you all know. I'm not sure what I did to deserve so many amazing people in my life and this experience has given me a whole new perspective on relationships. It's true what they say... Hard times will always reveal true friends. It's sad that it takes a life altering event to make you appreciate people and blessings but it's really making me thankful in a way that I'm going through this. The life lessons I am learning are invaluable and I'm grateful for that. After the pick up on Saturday I went to my dad's house and enjoyed some dinner with my family followed by a fire pit nightcap. It was the perfect day.

Yesterday was Mother's Day and we had some extended family come in town to spend it with us. I woke up with a headache but as I've mentioned in previous posts, I'm used to having headaches almost daily. The headache got worse throughout the day and by about 2 PM I was out of energy and ready to go home and rest. This morning I woke up with another headache, but it

18

was more of a pounding one this time. I took my extra strength Tylenol, as I usually do, without any improvement. Tried one of the stronger pain killers-still nothing. I had a group at work this morning that I needed to be in early for. They were storing items in my office and I needed to help make sure they were ready for their registration to begin. I had to push through the pain, paint on a grin, slap on the wig, and go in. Although most would say "you should have stayed home" I know that I personally would not be able to get any rest if I did not go into work for a few hours to make sure I got done what I needed to for the day. After about 4 hours I was comfortable with where I needed to be as far as daily priorities and my headache had only gotten worse. I was concerned this morning with the headaches. I know headaches are a side effect, not necessarily from the chemo cuz my last treatment was almost two weeks ago, but more from the implant last week. Still… Those should have only been for a couple days and it has now been a week since the implant. Just to be safe, my mom called the doctor to let them know about the headaches and asked if we should be concerned and/or if I needed to take other medications. My oncologist has ordered another MRI - this time for my brain. Both the initial MRI and most recent PET scans did not include specific pictures of the brain- they only targeted the other organs in my body besides the brain- not sure why. I will get that done tomorrow afternoon.

Wednesday morning I go in to get my second chemo treatment, and now to also get the results from my brain MRI. Since the cancer had spread to my collarbone, it's not impossible for it to have spread to my brain. The doctor said there's no reason to test for that UNLESS the patient notices ongoing headaches or other usual things... Which I had not been experiencing until recently. So, if you are sending up any prayers over the next day, please feel free to join me in praying that the cancer has not spread to my brain. Hopefully my body is still adjusting to all of the new drugs that have been pumped into it over the past couple of weeks and the headaches are just a way of my body saying "we are pissed at you for putting all these chemicals inside here Lindsay". Trust me, I'm not too happy about it either, body. Just continuing to take it one day at a time. I hope everyone enjoyed their Mother's Day weekend - more to come over the next couple days.

19

Diane: *Lindsay always had a strong work ethic; I believe thanks to us (her parents) modeling this characteristic. She had always given 110% to her job and wouldn't settle for less during this time. Even if she wasn't physically at work, she was working remotely on her computer. This was important to her as she never wanted to let anyone down. I think that as long as things remained as "normal" as possible, things would be ok. She was probably overdoing it at this point, but working and living life as normal as possible was SO important to Lindsay during this period. Our conversations revolved around her taking it easy and her work understanding what she was going through. Every day brought surprises, news (some good, mostly bad) and new ways of life. Those days are a blur in my memory. Not to diminish Lindsay's challenges in any way, but it was wearing on me.*

Doctor appointments, labs, x-rays, medication additions and changes, dealing with her side effects and test results - stressful doesn't begin to describe my days. And I was trying to run a business at the same time. Getting business done on a daily basis, sending emails, posting on social network, dealing with vendors and musicians and making sure the GL had staff coverage, sometimes at the last second when I had to help Lindsay. It's that work ethic thing again. I MUST make sure everything runs smoothly even if I wasn't there 50 hours a week, like usual. But, my priority at that time was Lindsay. Period. Thank God for Kevin and our amazing, flexible staff. Especially one named Deb Lee. She was always available and willing to cover for me when I asked. Maybe ONCE was she unable to help, even with a minute's notice. I can never thank them enough for helping us get through that period of time.

Lindsay's Post 5-11-16

Today is Wednesday, May 11th. I am at the doctor's office getting my second round of chemotherapy. I woke up this morning eager to find out the MRI results, and anxious about the side effects that I would feel after my second treatment. My MRI showed that my brain does NOT have any cancer in it!!! Thank you, God!!! They are thinking the headaches are from all of the hormonal changes and medications. My body has been thrown into this whirlwind out of nowhere. They also said these hormonal changes are the reason why my eyes got big when I looked at the scale this morning. I've gained ten pounds since my last treatment. 5 pounds since my last appointment last week. Not only did I go off my birth control pill after 10+ years, but I am going through menopause now- full force. It doesn't help that a lot of the pre-meds that they give me before the chemotherapy are steroids. I've never been this heavy in my life. I've been trying to eat healthy and have found myself eating less, especially when I was experiencing the nausea after the first treatment. I was confident that I had actually lost a couple pounds... HA! So, here is a new struggle that I will be dealing with - now I won't just be a bald lady, I'll be a plumped up bald lady. Oh well. My body image used to be something that I struggled with and normally if I would have gained ten pounds in two weeks I would probably start going to the gym every day and trying some crazy new diet. There's nothing I can do now except make sure to watch what I eat, and try not to focus on the way that I look. I know that the hormone treatment and the steroids are going to be worth it later. They also wanted to check my blood sugar and liver functions before I started my treatment today. We received word that those came back looking great. I think this is the first day since April 18th that I have been happy to be in a doctor's office. Minus the weight thing, I've only gotten good news since I've been here. Nothing in my brain, blood counts look good, sugar levels are good... And best of all, Doctor seemed really happy with the reaction my tumor had to the first treatment. Even though it looks bad on the outside still, he says that he's happy with the results and its "doing what it's supposed to" so he did not have to alter the recipe for my chemo today - same steroids and red devil. All positive news today. All of the prayers are working... Keep em coming!! Fingers crossed I will not have a bad reaction after today's treatment. #slaysquad

Diane: *Lindsay was definitely changing mentally, emotionally, and physically. Mentally and emotionally in good ways. Her appreciation for her family and friends had reached an all-time new level, she was keeping a positive mental attitude about her treatment and future, was eating healthy, spending as much time as possible with those she loved, avoiding the negative people trying to insert themselves into her life, reading the bible, and praying a lot.*

She had always been a crier, as are all the women in our family, but she wasn't crying much anymore. At least not in front of me. I believe she was taking her mental and emotional energy and putting it into her posts. But the weight gain, life-altering side effects from chemo and meds, and the unknowns were more than anyone should have to deal with.

21

Lindsay's Post 5-13-16

Today is Friday, May 13th. I had my second chemo treatment 2 days ago. I felt okay Wednesday evening and so-so Thursday morning. I went into work for a few hours yesterday morning. I woke up early- Wednesday night I didn't get much sleep for some reason. Thursday, I had to go back to get my Neulasta shot. I felt fine immediately following and into the evening. Went to bed early last night in anticipation of a full day at work today. Woke up this AM and my body was telling me NOPE, not today. My whole body felt sore, like I'd been hit by a bus. The nausea and headache accompanied the aches. Still feeling that way now. The Neulasta shot causes the bone pain- I had this same reaction 2 weeks ago. Went into work to get a few things done but didn't last longer than a couple hours. Hoping to feel better tomorrow.

Diane: *Even though Lindsay felt like crap most days she posted, she felt it was important to take a few minutes, even if it was a short post, to update everyone. She was reaching so many people through her writing and hundreds of people were waiting to hear from her. She had received so much love from so many she knows and so many people she'd never met. If she didn't post for a few days, people got worried and started reaching out to me. "Is Lindsay ok? We haven't seen a post for a while." It was like her mission. Researching IBC and looking for answers and/or other treatment options, and writing her posts as often as she could.*

Lindsay's Post 5-15-16

Today is Sunday, May 15th. Tomorrow will be the 1-month mark since my diagnosis. I can't believe what my body has gone through in the past 4 weeks. I've felt more pain physically, mentally, and emotionally in the past 4 weeks than I have in my entire life. It's still all very surreal to me. I am feeling better since my last post. Friday was not a good day at all. I did not leave my bedroom for over 24 hours between Friday-Saturday. It's almost like an intense flu virus feeling... sore, tired, nauseous. I thought some fresh air might help so I went over to my dad's house Saturday- early evening. We ended up getting dinner and I felt much better by the end of the day Saturday, but by about 8 PM I hit a wall and needed rest. I spent the majority of today in bed again, and by early afternoon I was feeling good enough to get outside, take the dog for a walk, and do some picking up around the house. What I would normally do naturally... Daily... takes so much energy. I went to my mom's house late this afternoon to grill out and got to spend some time with my brother, sister and niece who I hadn't seen in several days. I find myself feeling like days apart from loved ones seem like weeks. I am bummed I had to miss one of my besties gender reveal parties today. Sarah and Moe are having a BOY!! I hate having to miss out on things. It is hard to stay positive when it feels unfair to have to miss out on important things, and seeing important people... To not be in control. But life's not fair. And I need to get over it and focus on slaying. Good news- I didn't feel nauseous at all today. The body aches have improved significantly over the past 48 hours. The new issue - sore head. My doctor told me that when my hair started falling out it would come out in clumps. He also said when it started coming out it would happen quickly. It was supposed to happen 1-2 weeks after my first chemo treatment. I hit 2 weeks this past Wednesday and hadn't noticed any hair loss. For a moment It crossed my mind ... "Maybe I'm not going to lose my hair."... "Maybe I'm special."... I'm not "normal" and I'm kicking ass so maybe I'm not going to have to deal with that. It's past 2 weeks. I did it. Well, that was why I decided to buzz my head before it started falling out... I figured it would be easier/less messy to have 1-inch pieces of hair everywhere than huge fur balls. I also didn't think I would be able to mentally handle having handfuls of hair come out all at once one day in the shower. I'm so glad I made that decision. I wasn't an exception. My hair started coming out over the weekend when I was already at a very low point. I have to keep a scarf or chemo cap on my head at all times, so my head is really only exposed when I'm in the shower anyway. I only noticed that it had started coming out because the inside of one of my chemo caps was coated in little hairs when I took it off to get in the shower Saturday. I had been warned about my head getting sore or sensitive but had not experienced that until it started falling out. Today, I'm taking the extra strength Tylenol, not because of the body pains, but because of the sores on my head where patches of hair have come out. It's such a weird feeling. My eyebrows, which were already barely there, and my eyelashes.... My beautiful long lashes... Are Falling out now too. My lashes are MY THING! Well, they were. My scarves are my thing now. Thankfully, my hairs on my head are about the same length as my lashes and brow hairs; so I'm trying to pretend they're all head hairs when they land on my phone screen. My Amber Rose look is not as on fleek anymore- there are bald patches all over! Still got dat booty doh.

I hope everyone is having a nice weekend. I'm hoping to have the strength to get through the upcoming work week. No doctor appointments scheduled for this week. Fingers crossed that doesn't change and that my head sensitivity continues to be my only issue. Thank you to everyone who has tried to see me and has been checking up on me. Love you!

Diane: *"My scarves are my thing now." "Still got dat booty doh." Can you believe this girl? She kept up her positivity in her posts even when going though things you and I could never imagine. In person, though, with me, things were different. Don't get me wrong, Lindsay tried hard to stay positive and smile with me, too, but she knew she could be real with me. And she could take out her anger on me. We were closer than we'd ever been. Closer than any mom and daughter could possibly be. We both hated this. It really, really sucked. But I tried my best to keep her distracted, helped her plan so she could feel in control and even let her drive us to appointments, etc.,when she wanted to. We watched movies together, ordered food delivered and ate together, watched her favorite TV show at 6:30,* Wheel of Fortune, *and played the same game on our phones. She also enjoyed watching old Roseanne reruns. She rarely missed an episode. I also got hooked on* Orange is the New Black *on Netflix. I didn't get through all the seasons and couldn't bring myself to watch again after she passed away. It was our thing.*

Lindsay's Post 5-18-16
Today is Wednesday, May 18th. Yesterday was the first day in weeks that I made it through an entire work day! I woke up feeling fantastic and it lasted. I was even up for a glass of wine on my way home to celebrate! I stopped at my mom's store and had a glass. I hadn't had a glass of wine in a couple days and before that, I hadn't had one in several days. I'm not able to drink for at least 48 hours after chemo so that was why I didn't have any last week. And now I really just don't have the desire to drink like I did; which is a good thing I suppose. If you would have asked me 2 months ago if I would have to measure the quality of my day based on whether or not I could stay awake and function normally for an 8 hour period I would have laughed. If you would have asked me if I would go multiple days without a glass of wine, I

would find it equally as humorous. My days used to be jam packed with meetings, networking, socializing... From sun up to sun down most days. Your typical 28 year old, unattached, career-focused woman. Working only 8 hours was rare because it was always more than that. Now it's rare because my body won't allow it. I am hopeful that one day I will be able to have that kind of energy and normalcy back. Or is this a sign that I need to slow down?? I need to work less and enjoy life more? Focus on myself and being healthy? Am I supposed to be forming these habits while I'm sick because God wants me to live and live better? Or if I get better, will I go back to my fast-paced lifestyle? Will I get better??

I have always had anxiety and been a little OCD, but having cancer has brought the anxiety to a whole new level. I find myself constantly questioning "why" and "what if". My oncologist had prescribed a mild anxiety medication for me but I can't tell if it's working or not. I believe my increased anxiety has been part of the reason why I haven't been sleeping well. Last night I was so tired from my "long" day... Laid down for bed around 830 and was awake, tossing and turning until almost midnight. My body was so tired but my brain wasn't. Woke up at 5 AM this morning and couldn't go back to sleep. Almost every morning I'm waking up early for no reason. Previously I would hit snooze at least 2-3 times and have to peel myself out of bed in the morning. Is it because my brain can't shut off? I can't tell. But it's annoying. I hope I am able to get through my day today without being fatigued but I have a feeling the lack of sleep will catch up with me sooner than later.

(MEN: you may want to stop reading this post here as I am about to mention the words PERIOD and VAGINA)! Yesterday I began what I thought may be a period. With the hormone implant, the menopause and everything else, I did not think I was going to have one. Much like everything else, its side effects have been x10. Take your normal PMS and intensify. It is certainly not normal; extremely heavy, clotting, and today I'm feeling the cramping, bloating, etc way more than I ever have. Every day I wake up with no knowledge of what is going to unfold. I wasn't expecting to get a period- I was told I wouldn't get one. I wasn't expecting to start losing my hair over the weekend- I was past the point I was told it would fall out. I wasn't

25

expecting to celebrate having a good day yesterday- every day is different. Here's hoping today is another to celebrate. The sore head that I mentioned in my post on Sunday night has continued. In 3 days, I've lost about 3/4 of my hair. It is almost completely bald in the back now, with large patches everywhere else. It definitely makes it harder and a lot more uncomfortable to wear a wig every day and have the pressure on my sore head.

I shared a picture of my head with someone I love very much last night. Her response was this: "I don't know if this helps but it always makes me feel better when I think of this body as my shell. It is mortal and doesn't define my beauty. Outward beauty is superficial and fades your true beauty resonates from within and is shown in your character and deeds. And yours my love is stunning! You are a beautiful woman on the outside, gorgeous really. But that outward beauty can't hold a candle to your inner beauty. Truly! Love you to the moon." And that my friends, is how I am getting through my days. Thank you God for giving me the love and support of so many amazing people. Happy Hump Day!

Diane: *Communication Lindsay received, like the message at the end of her last post, TRULY helped her get through her worst days. Daily messages, texts, snail mail, hand-made cards from my cousin (who Lindsay had never met!), gift cards for McDonald's or Dairy Queen - all things she looked forward to on a daily basis. Visits, flowers, calls - all meant SO MUCH to her!*

Lindsay's Post 5-21-16
Today is Saturday, May 21st. It is a beautiful day! Unfortunately, I've spent it in bed :(I hope everyone else is out enjoying it!! I must have jinxed myself by hoping for a week without seeing my doctor because I ended up there on Thursday- boo!! I will spare you the details on this one... it is associated with an area where the sun don't shine- 'nuf said! Every time I think I've done all the research I can do on chemotherapy side effects, something comes out of left field that I hadn't heard about.

After a not-so-comfortable exam Thursday AM, we were relieved to know that there were no infections. I had my white blood cell count checked - all looked fine and I was sent home to rest. During chemo a main concern is your immune system not being able to fight infection with the drop in white blood cells. I've also learned that drinking "lots" of water is not just your typical 8 glasses per day. My body is needing as much water as possible, which isn't the easiest thing to focus on when you're sleeping so much. On the bright side- I had only gained 1 pound since I was there last week... Better than the 5 lbs/week that I had been used too- small victory!! Yesterday was great. I felt good all day. Thursday's bad day was the only one over a 4 day stretch- not bad!

Today has been spent in bed again, with a little intermission earlier to go out and water my new plants (thanks Dad and Mary!)- my yard is looking great. Wish I could be enjoying it now. I'm supposed to stay out of the sun which sucks and is so hard!! Normally I would have been parked on a patio somewhere taking in the rays with a few cold ones. So jeally of anyone who is doing that right now! On another note: Umm why didn't I watch Broad City sooner? Thanks to my friend Jenna who gave me her Hulu info, I was able to start watching today and I am obsessed. Lauren knew it. So funny!! The weezy references-I can't. Anyway....

We have some family coming in town tonight for my niece's baptism tomorrow. I've decided to pass on joining the festivities. I want (and need) to get as much rest as I can today and save my energy for tomorrow. Audrey Jean will be baptized at 11 am mass, followed by a little gathering for our family. I am hoping to wake up feeling good tomorrow so I can spend the day with loved ones.

Wondering about my hair? Almost completely bald now after a week! I am so shocked how quickly it came out. Only a couple little patches left! T-minus 4 days until my next chemo treatment which will be number 3 out of 12... 1/4 of the way through! Wishing everyone a relaxing weekend with loved ones. XO

Diane: *Missing out on activities and events was so hard for Lindsay. She didn't want to miss a single moment with family and friends, but some days it was just too difficult.*

27

Lindsay's Post 5-25-16

Today is Wednesday, May 25th. I am recovering from my treatment this morning. My doctor did a full exam today prior to treatment rather than just blood counts. My nurse asked me before he came in if I was on any new medications that they weren't aware of- after she took my vitals. I felt like something wasn't right. I never did end up figuring out why she asked me that. Clearly still having anxiety issues. My heart rate or blood pressure must have been different than normal. My doctor was (for the first time) able to actually feel where the tumor started and ended. Before, it was so large that the whole breast was too swollen and the tumor couldn't be measured. We are at 7 cm. Usually stage 3 breast cancer has a tumor that is about 3 cm on average. So it's still a monster! BUT at least now he will be able to measure it to check its progress which is cool. One more round of this awful dense dense chemotherapy on June 8th. After that, I will have a different recipe and my two-week treatment schedule may change. Anxious to see what the next round will make me feel like and how often I'll have to get it. I'm really hoping to speed this thing up, as I must see Drake in Des Moines with my Krilly for my bday in October #haveto. I've found that planning things in the future helps me with my coping. Gives me something to look forward to and holding onto hope. I find myself coming up with new coping methods every day.

Tomorrow we go back for that damn Nuelasta shot... This is the one that makes me feel real low with the bone aches on top of the nausea and headaches. They say that Claritin helps with the side effects of the Nuelasta. I started the Claritin today - hoping that taking it sooner may help it be more effective?? We will see. I need to find a new driver... Driving with Koster could potentially be adding to the nausea yikes LOL love ya mom. I also found out that I have to go back for another round of the hormone implant therapy next week so that sucks. Was hoping for a great week next week... I'm in my friend Rachel's wedding and need to be feeling great next Thursday-Saturday! I'm already having to miss the bachelorette party this weekend in Nashville. A trip I've been looking forward to for many, many months. The good news is I got to see Rachie today before she takes off with the crew tomorrow. She made tank tops for the group and added a pink ribbon for me and let me know I would be there in spirit. That meant a lot to me.

The past few days have been touch and go. Miss Audrey had a beautiful baptism Sunday and I'm so blessed that I was able to be there to see it. She didn't even cry when they put the water on her head! But she did spit her binkie in the holy water tub LOL that's one holy binkie. She's literally Nick/Tom's twin. I love her so much!!

Monday was an amazing day. Worked all day! No issues. Tuesday not so much - only made it a few hours at work. I just never know when my body's going to tell me it needs rest. Thank you to everyone who continues to be so supportive! The smallest gestures mean the world to me and I really appreciate you. Enjoy your evening!

Diane: *Little Audrey's baptism was awesome. She is the light of joy in our lives right now. Lindsay made it through. She was now looking forward to the next big event; her dear friend Rachel's wedding was on her mind.*

Lindsay's Post 5-28-16

Today is Saturday, May 28th. I've been in bed for the past 30 hours. It seems like the Neulasta shot, which I got on Thursday afternoon, is what is really giving my body a hard time. I was doing pretty good until yesterday. My nausea turned into actual dry heaving and the thought of even taking a sip of water made me sick. I was also overwhelmed with emotional distress. I figured it was just like when you are a little kid and you don't feel good you just whine and cry and get upset because you don't want to not feel good anymore. I went in to the doctor's office and got fluids + Dex and Ativan. One of my favorite nurses was there with us and she looked at me and told me that it's okay to not be so strong all the time. It was there in my little chemotherapy room that I wept with my nurse and my mom and it was definitely one of my darkest days yet. I'm not sure if it's the physical changes, if it's depression from having to spend so much time disconnected from my "real" life, or if it's just the hormones taking over again. But whatever it is, I am ready for it to get better. The "honeymoon" phase of my cancer has passed. All the attention, messages from folks I haven't heard from forever,

29

the outpouring of love and support It's all very encouraging. But it fades and it's getting harder and harder to stay positive. I'm not writing this today to be negative but my favorite nurse's words about strength gave me the courage to share the struggles that I'm dealing with. I'm confident that by now there are several people that aren't interested in my daily thoughts and progress. At first it was almost like "omg this normal girl got this horrible disease" and it was entertaining. Well now it's getting real and part of my journey and sharing this blog with those who are interested is about transparency. I am not positive every day. My jokes and laughter aren't present all day every day unfortunately.

When I look in the mirror, I usually see tears in my reflection, not smiles. I can't paint a picture that this awful experience is always going to have a positive spin of hope and strength. I promise to do all that I can to be the positive and strong person that I know I am. But I am also human and this shit is terrible. It's important to me to capture the bad days too. Here are a couple verses from 2 Corinthians that I am connecting with: But He said to me, "My grace is sufficient for you, for my power is made perfect in weakness." Therefore, I will boast all the more gladly of my weaknesses, so that the power of Christ may rest upon me. For the sake of Christ, then, I am content with weaknesses, insults, hardships, persecutions, and calamities. For when I am weak, then I am strong."

Diane: *It was definitely starting to get harder for Lindsay to stay positive. She was still trying her best to keep a smile on her face, or at least disguise her anguish and depression. It was like pulling a window shade down over her face, at least in front of others - except me.*

Lindsay's Post 5-30-16
Today is Monday, May 30th... Memorial Day 2016! My day started off well. I was feeling okay-good enough to get out of bed. Headache and nauseated but nothing out of the ordinary. I watered my plants, put up my umbrella on the patio and had two special friends come to visit me this morning. It was the first time since last week that I have felt up for getting out of bed to have a visitor just stop by. AND I got to FaceTime with baby AJ after that!! My mom came by and did some cleaning around my house for me, too. All of

this activity took place between 8-Noon. By about 1 PM I was over the toilet. I had not eaten anything so there wasn't much that was coming up which makes the experience way worse. The dry heaving has made my throat raw. Water still sounds awful all the time. I used to crave water... Like I could chug an entire bottle in one sitting and it would taste so amazing. Especially on a hot day like today. When I was first diagnosed people had told me that my taste buds would get weird and that water would taste bad. I always thought that was probably one of many situational opinions and that it wouldn't happen to me cuz I love drinking water and water has no taste so how the heck could it taste BAD?! It just didn't sound right. But it's a real thing! Much like everything else I'm experiencing, it is hard to describe. Impossible really. Still- I'm drinking as much as I can when I can because I know that it is important to stay hydrated.

Tomorrow I am planning on going into work in the morning then I have to go back for my second round of the hormone therapy implant tomorrow afternoon. They give me a local anesthetic before injecting the implant (little disc) under the skin near my belly button. They compare the pain of the implant to a "bee sting".. I've never been stung by a bee and I have a feeling whoever came up with that comparison hasn't either.

Thank you to all of those who have served our country and congratulations to everyone who graduated this weekend. I know that I had to miss several gatherings and opportunities to see loved ones again this weekend but please know that I appreciate all of the inclusion and invitations that I'm still getting to things. Even though I can't attend, just knowing that I am in my friend's and family's thoughts means a lot to me!! I shared a video earlier on Facebook about a man who captured his wife's battle with breast cancer through photographs and it really hit home for me. He made a valid point that sometimes it is hard for those that love a cancer patient to understand what the family and patient are going through on a daily basis. I try to share all the pertinent information through my posts but it truly is different actually being there and living it. I know the difficulty in communicating the emotions is mutual. It is difficult to find the "right" words to say to me or my parents or brother, I know. "I'm sorry" and "you're in my prayers" are the normal things to say. Those simple words mean so much to us, even if you

31

feel like they don't. There's not much more to say than that. A look, a smile, a hug, a kind gesture, a note... Those things are just as meaningful. I know I say this in my posts often but it's because I mean it... I really truly appreciate every single person that has reached out and shown support. The truth is- there's nothing anyone can do except for continue to love us. In the video, the husband mentioned that his wife felt most supported by her friends when they just sat together and held her hand. To my besties: when I'm not able to see you, it's not because I don't want to and your efforts do not go unnoticed. When I don't respond to a text or call it's because I mentally or physically am not able to talk to you. The more I love you the harder it is. But knowing that you called or texted means more than you know. Thank you #slaysquad for continuing to give me life and hope every day! That's all for now- I hope everyone has a great evening and start to another work week. XOXO

Diane: *Lindsay started the whole* #slaysquad *movement at the beginning of her cancer life. Like "slaying the dragon". And she loved Beyonce's song* Formation. *She* slays *a lot in that song. Lindsay's daily mantra was "Wake, Pray, Slay" and she was trying to live it every day. She was consumed with* cancer. *Watching cancer-related movies, searching online about cancer, reading about cancer. It became her entire focus most days. Trying to drink, eat, rest. Dealing with different side effects each day. Wondering about her future. Is she going to lose her hair, going to be able to have children one day, going to live or die? I have to admit this all applied to me, as well. The* EXACT SAME THINGS.

Lindsay's Post 6-5-16
Today is Sunday, June 5th. As many have seen from my Facebook posts, my prayers for getting through Rachel's wedding weekend were answered! The festivities began Thursday night when we had spray tans at my house. My mom came over and helped me set up and be there in case things went south for me and I needed help hosting. The opposite happened. It seemed like the moment my friends began arriving, I had a burst of new energy and ended up sitting outside catching up with friends until almost 11 PM!

Friday I took the day off of work to prep for the wedding and get as much rest as I could before the rehearsal. I ended up going in to work anyway for a couple hours that morning and rested in the afternoon. Besides being a little tired and super hot (damn menopause) I made it through the rehearsal without any issues. Saturday we had to be at the salon by 8 AM and my morning started off with a headache but by the time we got to the church for the wedding I was feeling great. I used my human hair wig and also added my Halo in to the wig for styling, which I hadn't tried before. It worked out perfectly. I was afraid I wouldn't be able to do anything fancy with the wig and extensions but it worked! I decided to do a side braid and curls to have my hair cover the scar where my port is on the left side of my chest. I even had eyebrows, lashes, and everything. I looked like my old self! My hair was the same length again as it was before I cut off 11 inches a month ago... Pre-hair loss. I had planned on probably not being able to stay for the reception. Not only did I stay for the reception but I enjoyed cocktails and danced and partied and had the time of my life with all my best friends! For one night, I forgot I was sick. I feel like myself. I felt HAPPY! It was awesome!!!! And much needed. I haven't smiled like that in months. Thank you, God for giving me the opportunity to enjoy myself so much! I am paying for it today though. Every bone in my body is sore and I have already taken 3 naps!! But it was worth it. The memories are priceless!

Tomorrow I will work in the AM and then have a class at Genesis in the afternoon called "Look Good, Feel Better", a cancer patient seminar that was recommended for me to learn how to deal with the many physical changes that my body is going through. I'm sure I will be half the age of most of my classmates but am still looking forward to it. The more educated I can be, the better. Also, the #slaysquad t-shirts (second order) are in!!! Tomorrow my brother is picking them up for me. If you ordered a shirt, you will be able to get it from me this week! Details to come on good pick up place/times. If anyone is wanting a shirt that didn't order one, I did get a few extra so please let me know if you're interested!

This Wednesday I will receive my 4th and final dense dose of the Adriamycin chemotherapy - the "red devil" which has kicked my butt. I will then begin the Taxol round of chemo, which could be every 2 weeks x 4 just like the Adriamycin was OR it could be administered weekly x 12. My doctor will determine the dosage and/or changes as he goes along, depending on how I respond to the therapy. Much like the first round, this one will take about

2 ½ - 3 hours each time I believe. Also like the current recipe, the white blood count will be affected, so will use Neulasta to help WBC's recover. A lot of the Taxol side effects seem similar to the ones I'm having after the chemo now, so it will be interesting to see what changes. Prayers that I respond well to the new drug so we can keep things moving. Stay tuned! Hope everyone had a great weekend.

Diane: *Well, she made it through one of the most important weekends of her illness. Her friend, Rachel's wedding. I was holding my breath all weekend, expecting to get a call to come get her. I texted her several times to check in and she was always doing well. What a relief! She was so concerned about her dress fitting due to her weight gain, but a little alteration and it was fine. She looked beautiful in her wig and full makeup. And the biggest smiles :) On to the next thing....a new chemo recipe and getting through the warm summer with her menopause symptoms.*

Lindsay's Post 6-8-16
Today is Wednesday, June 8th. I am currently sitting at the oncology office getting my 4th dense dose of chemotherapy. I was able to give doc his slay squad shirt- he loved it. He is the slay master!! The connection that I have with my doctor is special and I couldn't be happier with my decision to stay in the Quad Cities for treatment. Doctor didn't measure the tumor size today but we continue to be very pleased with how I've been responding to the medicine. As mentioned in my previous post, this is the last round of the red devil recipe- Adriamycin and Cyclophosphamide + Doxorubicin.

Tomorrow I will have my Neulasta shot as usual to follow up today's treatment and increase WBCs. Next week I will have a week off to rest and complete the absorption of the 4th red devil dose and then I will start a new cycle, which will be weekly for 12 weeks. I knew that I would be getting the Taxol drug but I found out today that doctor wants to add another drug called Carboplatin to the recipe. Carboplatin is used in treatment for other types of cancers, but has recently been used in clinical studies to be helpful with breast cancer. Why not add another drug, right?! So now my medication list will include Ativan, Dexamethasone, Dibucaine, Ondansetron, Prochloperazine, Sertraline, Doxorubicin, Cyclophosphamide, Neulasta, Palonosetron, Diphenhydramine, Goserelin plus ES Tylenol, OTC meds, and now 2 more chemotherapy meds. The list continues to grow! I will have the 3-4 hour push every Wednesday starting on June 22nd and ending on September 7th. June 21st I will go in for more labs. Surgery will take place about 3-4 weeks after we are done with the 12 week plan. That falls right on my birthday AND Drake concert... Ugh. Guess I might be spending my 29th birthday in the hospital.. but such is life! I will be glad to see another birthday and that's all that I'm focused on. I will not get too discouraged until we have a surgery date set in stone. Fingers crossed it will all work out according to my preferences as far as surgery dates but this is just another reminder that as much as I want to control everything around me, I just can't. After surgery, I will begin radiation. Also, during this time, I will get some more genetic testing done. It was nice to have a little bit more of a "schedule" as far as treatments, surgery and radiation for the next several months. That takes some of the anxiety away from me. What isn't helping my anxiety is the fact that I will probably need to make a change as far as work goes, now that I know that I'll have to have chemo every week through the fall. I'm not sure how that will work, but I am going to try not to think about it or worry about it now. The Carboplatin drug that they're going to add to the Taxol is one that intensifies the metallic taste in my mouth. They said that I should start using plastic silverware to avoid the harshness of the metal taste. Most of the side effects will stay the same for the next chemo recipe besides that, but the Taxol will also be a little bit tougher on my blood counts. They will not give me the Neulasta shot after my first round of the new drug because they want to see how my WBC's hold up. If my white blood counts don't drop too significantly, they may not give me the Neulasta, but we will see how I react. Also, for the Taxol, I am going to have to take steroid pre-meds the day before and morning of my treatments. I gained about 20 pounds in the first few weeks of chemotherapy from steroids. My weight has stopped increasing... THANK GOD! But I'm not sure if the steroids that I'll be taking more frequently with the new recipe will cause for more fluctuation. The reason the steroids are required for the Taxol is because many have allergic reactions to it. I suppose I can deal with gaining a few more pounds if it means saving my life. I've only got about an hour left this morning and then will spend the afternoon resting.

Tomorrow, of course, Neulasta shot in the AM. Friday I'm supposed to be going to see Lil Wayne with my friends... we are all wearing colored wigs to pretend we are Nicki Minaj. I really, really, really, really hope that I am feeling good enough to go....even if only for part of it. Then Saturday AM is Race for the Cure! I am not supposed to be in the sun so I don't know yet if I will go through with the 5k or not. I usually have my worst few days Thurs-Sun following treatment so I know that my plans may be changed depending on how it goes this week. Thank you for your continued prayers!!

Diane: *The amount of information and education we all received during this time was massive. Definitely on information overload! Medical terminology, cancer treatment regimens, drugs names, etc... I would always take notes when we were at the oncology clinic, so that I could report to Tom and Nick, but also so that Lindsay would have accurate information for her posts. It was important to her to share as much education and information as possible, to keep people up to date...but also, I think it was another way she could feel some control over her situation. At that time, she was feeling some control as she understood what was being done and what the plan was for the short term. Little did we know that things weren't going to go as planned.*

Lindsay's Post 6-13-16
Today is Monday, June 13th. I just woke up for my second nap of the day. This came on the heels of 1.5 days spent resting. Wednesday went well after round 4 of chemo and Thursday I had my shot and began feeling the side effects that night. I woke up Friday with the aching body, but I could tell that my conscious effort to pre-medicate had worked. I started the nausea and allergy meds a couple days earlier than I had been, which really helped. Thank you, Shari for the suggestion! I soaked in the tub and rested up all day Friday in order to catch a glimpse of Weezy. It was fun but definitely took a lot out of me. Saturday morning, I went to Race for the Cure, but did not participate. I engaged in the survivor photo and pre-race festivities, had some breakfast with my friends and family who came out to support me, and by 10 AM I was ready to crash. I spent the rest of the weekend "recovering".

My friend Mary Beth brought me a lovely care package a couple weeks ago and included some of those Dasani water flavoring things and they have helped me to drink more water!! I had expected to feel good today after getting plenty of rest and hydration. Uh uh. This morning I woke up feeling nauseous and was experiencing the same "sun don't shine" issue that I mentioned a couple weeks ago. Sucks!! But I knew I had to go into work because it was important for me to discuss my schedule going forward after finding out that my chemo treatments will be weekly starting next Wednesday through September. The sickness I felt may have been brought on from the anxiety of that realization. Work is, and has been, my life for the past 5 years. Before that in college, it was school and work. Before that in high school, sports and school and work. I've always had a strong work ethic and have always been someone who is busy all the time. The thought of not working is an extremely hard pill for me to swallow. I can say that this is the second worst part of being sick (first is still the hair loss/physical changes). Not having a paycheck for several months, and more importantly, not having the human interaction and engagement that I live for seems like the worst thing possible. How will I pay for this, how am I going to do that, how will the world go on without me working? It will. But I know that I need to spend my time away from the everyday stressors of work and allow my body to rest if I want to beat this thing. I don't think I'm depressed but I do know that my battle seems to get more difficult every day. I pray that one day I will get back to living the life that I love... Back to being "me". I am constantly reminded of my misfortune. It seems like every time I turn on the TV or radio or scroll through social media, I'm constantly hearing about cancer. Literally every five seconds. Was it always this way or am I just more aware of it now? The thought hit home for me after the recent devastation in Orlando. Do we subconsciously tune out the bad things going on around us until we are affected by them? Do we let things get worse and worse and worse until lives are taken and we are left wondering what we could have done differently? Do we ignore the warning signs? It is extremely disheartening and makes me question this world that we are living in. Why do bad things happen to undeserving people? Why are we separated from loved ones who are taken from us too soon? My faith tells me that one day I will have answers to these questions and in the mean time I must trust in God. Life is not fair. For me, it's not about the politics. It is just another reminder that life is short and we should never take one single day for granted. We can try to figure out "why" but the distress of that loaded question is overbearing. We all plan for the best, right? We save our money but still come across financial struggles at some point. We put all of our trust and love into a relationship and end up getting disappointed. We exercise, watch our diet and strive for healthiness and are stricken with illness. We are constantly shaking our proverbial fist at some point in our life saying "this isn't fair!!!" And "why me?!". We must focus on the positive and remember that we all face struggles. Rather than dwelling on them and playing victim we should focus our energy on change. All we can do is love one another and hold on to hope. Proverbs reminds us to trust in the Lord with all our hearts and lean not on our own understanding.

The next week for me will be spent out of the doctor's office (fingers crossed) and I will be preparing my body and mind for the second round of chemo medications. I will also focus on praying for others who are experiencing turmoil much greater than mine. Be grateful, tell your loved ones how much they mean to you. Life can change in the blink of an eye. Today- I'm breathing. For that, I have no complaints. XOXO

Diane: *Lindsay was such a trooper at the Susan G. Komen Race for the Cure. I couldn't help but reminisce about the years I was involved as a volunteer, when the kids were little, and how I never would have thought my little girl would be stricken with this disease. I pulled out pictures of the kids wearing their race t-shirts and came across a photo of Lindsay joining in the Jazzercise warm-up before the race started. She was only 8, and so intent on getting the moves right, there to support her mommy.*

The Orlando devastation she refers to in her last post was a mass shooting at Orlando's Pulse nightclub during the early morning hours of June 12, 2016. The worst mass shooting in U.S. history, according to the media. There were 49 people killed, and 53 more hospitalized while simply having fun during Pride month. A true act of terror and hate that shook Lindsay to her core. She loved ALL of her friends, many who are part of the LGBTQ community, and simply could not wrap her head around what had happened.

Lindsay's Post 6-19-16
Today is Sunday, June 19th... Father's Day 2016! I just got home after spending the evening in LeClaire with my dad and Mary. I am getting ready to fill up my pill box for the week, as I normally do on Sunday evenings...

(The pill box makes me feel so old!!). Yesterday was spent in Galena celebrating my cousins wedding. It has been so wonderful to spend the weekend with loved ones. I am reflecting tonight on how blessed I am to have such an amazing family. I got home at about 11 PM last night and needless to say I was exhausted and rested for most of the day today. Last week I worked every single day! It felt normal. It felt great. There were several moments over the past few days that I forgot I was sick. I have not felt that way for months. No issues and no unexpected doctor visits. Besides some exhaustion throughout the week, the past 7 days have been very good overall! I'd say the worst part about being out of house and feeling well is having to wear a wig all the time. When I'm in the house I do not wear it. When it's 90 degrees out, it is NOT fun!! Add that to the constant hot flashes and it makes for a very sweaty me!! But it's all good. I know people say "just don't wear the wig out!" I don't always. Sometimes I will just wear a scarf. But sometimes it's nice to look and feel like my old self, even if just a little bit. I am so thankful to be feeling well! I have not taken one day for granted and have been thanking God every day this past week for the strength that I've been given.

I am looking forward to starting my new chemo recipe this Wednesday. I am hoping for this next 12 week cycle to pass by quickly! Am also hoping that I respond well to the treatment and do not have as many side effects this go around, or new ones that I am not expecting. I will post an update later this week after my treatment of course. Thank you for your ongoing prayers and positive thoughts!!!

Diane: *Lindsay really did hate wearing the wig, but felt she needed to – not for herself, but for others that were uncomfortable seeing her "sick". Having no hair is like a flashing billboard saying "I have cancer" and Lindsay equated that to "feel sorry for me", which she never wanted. Trying to get through days at work was wearing on her, and not just due to the heat and wearing the wig, but trying to be "normal" as much as she could, again more for others than for herself. But it just got to be too much.*

Lindsay's Post 6-24-16

Today is Friday, June 24th. It has been a long week so far, but not bad. I've spent a majority of the past couple days in bed. Tuesday was my official "last

39

day" at work until September. I have decided to take a 12 week leave of absence now that I have started weekly chemotherapy infusions. If all goes as planned, my last treatment would be September 7th and I'd return to work on the 12th. There would then be a couple weeks of "down time" before my mastectomy and radiation. It will be interesting to see how all of that plays out. I had been struggling with feeling like I needed to be at work full time on the days that I was able to be there. That just was not possible for me. The anxiety of feeling like I had to do something when I wasn't up for it was weighing heavily on me and it was a personal decision that made the best sense for me right now. I know that focusing on getting better is all that is important anymore. I am super lucky to have Lauren my colleague to help me feel good about being away for the next several weeks. She has been a saint and I am so, so thankful for her!

After my last half day Tuesday morning, I went in to get blood drawn at the doctor's office that afternoon. I don't think I've ever seen that big of a syringe full of blood. It was weird! Or maybe that's normal and I just usually don't look? Idk. And it is crazy how quickly they were able to extract that much blood in such a short time through my port. I try not to watch because it makes me queasy. The nurse then split it up into smaller containers and sent them off to the lab. I'm so glad that I was able to get a port. I see lots of old people in the chemo rooms with me who have to get stuck through their veins in arm/hands. Even though the port needle is thick and does hurt, It could be worse! Getting stuck with needles over and over all the time and not having them inserted tightly is not fun! Plus it seems like nobody could ever find my veins before. When they accessed my port Tuesday afternoon to take the labs I asked to keep the needle in there overnight so they wouldn't have to stick me again Wednesday AM. I didn't sleep well with the port accessed and taped up on Tuesday night but for me, I'd rather not sleep well than have to get my port poked again after being sore!! It makes me feel nauseous every time they access it.

We got to the doctor's office around 8:30 Wednesday morning. My doctor did a full body exam and we went over what the next 12 weeks would look like. Although my tumor has shrunk overall and "has edges" now, the breast is still red and is not "normal" looking compared to the other, which is the goal we are trying to reach! Even though we can't see inside the breast, we can tell by the outside if the medicine is working, I think. A chunk of the time spent with the doctor Wednesday morning was to go over genetic testing and a lot of it was foreign to me. I had mentioned in a previous post that they were giving me a drug that is being tested for my type of cancer in a clinical study right now. Since I'm triple negative, there is nothing specific for us to target.

It will take 2-3 weeks to get back the results of the additional genetic testing that we did Wednesday and depending on those results, Doctor may stop the additional drug. I got the feeling that the genetic stuff wouldn't matter. The nurse asked us a lot of questions about our family history. There is no history of cancer in our family so that convo was short lived. We have some heart stuff and some diabetes but no cancer. I think my doctor, much like all of us, really wants to figure out how and why this happened to me, at such a young age. The million-dollar question. It will be interesting to see what information comes back from those tests and whether there are any mutations.

I had to take two Dex steroids Tuesday PM and two more before going in on Wednesday. They began my pre-meds around 10 and pumped in even more Dex. I was worried that I may experience some of the confusion and blurred vision that I had last time I took all that Dex but I seemed to react fine. The nurse watched me closely as they pushed the Taxol. I did not notice any allergic reactions. I did get flushed and had some crazy hot flashes throughout but that is somewhat a regular occurrence so I didn't think much of it. I'm at the point where I say "F it" and take my scarf/cap off my head the moment I feel like I'm getting flushed. I don't really care who stares at me anymore. We ended up being at the doctor's office until almost 3 pm Wednesday... About 6 hours. I felt kind of weird after. Not nauseous or dizzy or anything like that but more mentally off. I think I was irritable and exhausted. I took some meds and went to bed early.

Yesterday was fine. I took a couple naps throughout the day but was strong enough to get out and run a couple errands. No Neulasta this time!! At all. Since my treatments are weekly, they monitor my WBCs enough where I don't need the Neulasta. This means that I will need to be even more careful about where I go, who I'm around, etc. I will need to keep sanitizer on me at all times and avoid infection. Today I've just been drained! Not feeling the best. I have been sleeping for the majority of the day. I am not feeling the sore bones and aches like they said I might but plan on taking a preventative hot bath this evening. I have felt a little itchy and have had a reoccurring throb in the left front part of my head. Overall, these symptoms have been much more tolerable than feeling like I'm going to barf all the time and have been hit by a bus like I was used to. Sleeping most of the day feels like such a waste but again, I know that I need to listen to my body and rest when I'm tired. It will be interesting to see if tomorrow is better or worse. I am hoping to be plenty rested before my benefit on Sunday!

One thing I've noticed, and my readers may begin noticing as well, is that "chemo brain" has been setting in. It's not necessarily a true medical term, I don't think, but basically people have reported having mind cloudiness throughout and after treatments. It's frustrating for me to get through this post right now because my brain just doesn't seem to be working as well as it normally does. I have to stop and really think about the words I'm typing- it used to come naturally and just flow. It is not a fun feeling. I feel like I'm losing control of a lot of things I never thought I would. I wanted to mention this in today's post because my lack of wit or goofiness may make it seem like I'm "not myself"... It's true, I'm not feeling like myself at all. I don't know if I'll ever feel like myself again. But that doesn't mean that I'm not hanging in there! And I want to keep posting so you will have to hang in there with me too. I might be repeating myself or not making sense sometimes but I have gotten so many positive comments on my posts so I will definitely not be stopping them. Happy Friday- I hope everyone has a nice weekend and maybe I will see you Sunday!

Diane: *I want to tell you more about the benefit Lindsay refers to in her last post, and in her next post. SLAY DAY, June 26, 2016, was a day that will forever be etched in my memory as one of the most amazing, fun, and love-filled days I've ever experienced. Nick helped Lindsay's friend Rachel plan the event held at the Public House in Davenport. The owners, Johnna and Austin, are good friends of Nick's who loved Lindsay to pieces and offered to help us put on this fundraiser at their business. So many others helped, attended, donated and simply SHOWED UP to support our fighter.*

As the crowd overflowed onto the patio, the staff of Public House were kept busy serving the hundreds of people who were there to raise money and show love to Lindsay. Our family, friends, neighbors and co-workers blessed us with their presence. To say it was an incredible testament to Lindsay would be an understatement. At the end of the day, we were ALL filled with such joy and appreciation. Those of you who participated and are reading this now, THANK YOU from the bottom of my heart.

Lindsay's Post 6-29-16
Today is Wednesday, June 29th. It is so weird that I have to look at the calendar in my phone to even know what the date is for sure. My dad reminded me that us non-working peeps seem to have an issue with never knowing what day is it LOL!! And it's only been a week. I spent a good chunk of my 4 hour treatment today archiving emails on my laptop. Still trying to adjust to my new schedule and priorities. The treatment went well overall. I am definitely not feeling the immediate side effects with my new cocktail. It is safe to say that this round is way less painful than the red devil. I was feeling well enough to have lunch and visit my niece after we were finished today. Have been laying low and feeling okay ever since. Trying to stay hydrated. I ran out of my Dasani drops and Mary has put me on to those flavored antioxidant drinks calls "Bai". The Kwik Star on Kimberly and Division has like 10 different flavors available. I definitely recommend trying these if you haven't!

As many already know, my guilty pleasure is anything Bravo TV. Primarily all the Real Housewives shows. I'm resting now, getting ready to get to sleep for the night, and watching RHONY. One of the characters Bethany had to get surgery and put together a living will. She broke down because she doesn't have parents or siblings or any immediate family to be with her. It just made me realize how thankful I am to have such a big family around me, and that no matter how successful you are, life is not complete without family. My mom takes me and sits with me through every 4-6 hour chemotherapy infusion... every week. My dad makes time in his very busy day to get away from the office and come see me during every single treatment. How depressing would it be if I had to go through this alone?

The benefit this past Sunday was a huge success! Like I'm still in shock about it. People that I love drove hours. Several miles, just to come give me a hug or look in my eyes on Sunday. People who could have been being productive with kids or yard work on a sunny summer weekend gave up that important time to spend the afternoon with me. It was 90 + degrees. People were drenched in sweat and packed in the venue shoulder to shoulder and they stayed. With smiles on their faces. I could go on and on about how amazing and unreal it was to me but will not beat a dead horse. I'm sure everyone is sick of hearing about slay day! (Insert one final Thank You).

I don't know what in the hell I've done to deserve so much love and kindness from so many people. Seriously- It's mind boggling. As much as this whole life or death situation that I'm dealing with sucks, I've never ever been so humbled and positive and happy in my heart, or even close to it. I am touched and so overwhelmed with gratitude to be getting the support that I literally couldn't live without. Everything happens for a reason. My cancer is making me view the world in a completely different way and I am thankful for the struggle because once I fight this, I am going to live my life differently forever. You always hear things and see quotes about "life's short" or "carpe diem". You know you're supposed to live by the golden rule blah blah blah. Like for example: I don't give a shit about someone cutting me off in traffic anymore. If someone needs to get into my lane... (Even tho it was rude as hell for them to speed all the way up until they are forced to merge rather than getting in the line a mile back and waiting like a good citizen)-it's not going to do anything but delay my commute by 10 seconds. And give that person the "I do what I want and I'm invisible" affirmation they were so longing for. Normally I'd consider hugging the bumper of the car in front of me just to send a big F U to that jerk. Who the hell gives a shit about something so dumb when you are literally fighting for your life? These are the things I notice every minute of every day and constantly catch myself feeling super awesome for having these realizations about the simplicity of the world being a better place. I know I will live such a more kind, slowed down, appreciative, patient, loving and happy life without giving one ounce of energy to the small things that most people normally just do naturally... Like sit on their horn or flick off the old person who can't drive, or not let them over like I would have considered doing before. I honestly do not have

44

the time or energy to give to anybody or anything but myself. The drama, the stress, the negativity... And I feel free. I dare you to try to live differently and be more cognizant of the small unimportant things that stress us out every day. I would ask those who are praying for me daily to switch out their prayer tonight and pray for those who are unhappy and adding to the coldness in this world. Those who are lost and thrive on negativity, hurtfulness, selfishness, disrespecting themselves, and settling for anything less than they deserve. Pray for those who need love in their hearts. Someone had prayed for that for me in some capacity and God answered that prayer in a unique and bold way. His ways are mysterious and I feel blessed. Challenge accepted big guy. Thank you all! If you have your health- your daily lives should be filled with joy and appreciation! Enjoy your holiday weekend with loved ones!! XO

Diane: *It seems, in hindsight, that this weekend was a turning point for Lindsay. Like a giant light bulb had turned on. She'd come to realize how much people truly loved her and were scared to lose her. People just wanted to see and hug her. She'd gained some new insight into the world and felt compelled to write about it. She'd become closer to God and placed her life in His hands.*

Lindsay's Post 7-2-16
Today is Saturday, July 2nd. I just took Lola for a walk around the neighborhood and it was the first time I've left the house today! It was kind of sad to see all of the family gatherings and parties going on. I am definitely missing out on the summer. Drinks, laughs, fireworks, memories being made. I strolled by the parties in my Victoria Secret pajama pants and t-shirt- probably staring and smiling at people like a creep.

Friday morning I woke up not feeling the best. I had a sore throat that got worse throughout the day and had a fever that was lingering on and off for over 24 hours. I'm currently at a 98.7 temp and my throat is feeling much better. I slept for almost 17 hours straight; only getting up a couple times to let the dog out. I must have caught a little cold. I hope this will not be a normal thing now that I do not get the Neulasta. I'm just glad that it seems to be getting better and not worse! Spending the holiday weekend in bed is so not fun :(I am totally feeling sorry for myself right about now. Jealous of everyone vacationing with family and enjoying the weather. Really hoping to feel better and can get out tomorrow for a bit! Hope everyone is enjoying their 4th of July weekend so far.

Diane: *I know she was looking forward to some kind of normalcy this weekend. Unfortunately, each day was different, and she never knew how she was going to feel or what she would be up to doing. She really tried not to feel sorry for herself, but I knew she was struggling with this.*

Lindsay's Post 7-4-16
Today is Monday, July 4th! Independence Day 2016. I spent the rest of my Saturday night laying low and getting more rest. Woke up Sunday feeling pretty good! No fever and my throat was not sore anymore. It was very strange how the pain came and went so quickly. One of the common side effects of chemo is mouth sores. Fortunately, I have not experienced these, but we are thinking that my sore throat may have been a side effect from the Taxol chemotherapy. We will have to check with the doctor on Wednesday. Still having lots of hot flashes. I was feeling good enough to go out for a bit last night and experience a glimpse of the 4th of July festivities that I'd so longed for!

My mom and Kevin picked me up around 8 and we headed to downtown Davenport to catch the fireworks. They were awesome!! It was a wonderful time. When I got home my body was so exhausted but my brain was not. I tossed and turned all night and did not get any sleep until I took an Ativan around 3 AM. Even then, I only stayed asleep for a couple hours. I racked my brain trying to figure out what the issue was and realized that I had started a higher dose of the Zoloft that morning. I had started at 25 mg a couple months ago, then 50, and now 100. Hopefully the increased dose is what is causing the restlessness and my body adjusts quickly. It is the worst feeling when you are so tired physically but wide awake mentally. Another thing I will need to talk to my doctor about this week.

This morning we went to my dad and Mary's house to have brunch and celebrate dad's birthday. I got to see the babies and Lola got to run around with Callie... or as Maya says "khaki". It was a really great time. After being outside for a couple hours I got pretty stuffed up and needed to head home. Now even though my throat is okay, I feel like I have symptoms of a head cold. I don't feel sick I just can't breathe well. Allergies? What else is going to happen to my body?! It seems like every day something new! Fingers crossed my WBCs aren't low and that we are able to move along appropriately on Wednesday. I'm noticing more of my eyebrows slowing coming out. I had read that the Taxol loosens up the last of the brow/lash hairs over the 12 weeks of treatment. I had stopped doing research for a while.

When I was first diagnosed (actually before I was diagnosed, deep down I somehow already knew) I had been researching IBC for hours upon hours every day. It consumed me. For the past month or so that I've been going through treatment, I haven't been researching as much but I'm starting to get back into it. Initially, I was researching IBC in general... What it is, how it's treated, other people's stories, etc. My biggest thing was making sure that I made the best decision as far as treatment in a short amount of time. Many people recommend MD Anderson in Texas for treatment, as they have doctors that specialize in IBC. I also wanted to see what was out there as far as clinical studies. I knew my case was so rare and could be used for doctors to learn more. I chose to stay here and be with my family and in my own home. Not only because it would be the most comfortable and "normal" for me, but also because I knew that the chemo, surgery, radiation schedule was going to be the same regardless as far as type of treatment. Now that I'm on my way with the treatment and have the "plan" for the next couple of months, it's time for me to dig into more about the hormones, receptors and my triple negative diagnosis. I am getting anxious to get back the additional genetic testing this week. I understand that since I'm triple negative, there is nothing specific for the doctors to target with my treatment. IBC is the most aggressive form of breast cancer, but being triple negative makes the prognosis even worse. IBC triple negative folks treated at MD Anderson in more recent years show a 50% chance of staying alive for up to 2 years and a 42% chance of making it 5 years, while the other IBC subtypes (positive receptors) have a significantly higher survival rate. It seems like I somehow keep getting the most uncommon, unimaginable additions to the already unreal statistics since diagnosis. Most of the blogs I've read from other women with triple negative IBC are no longer living. I don't like to talk about my slim chance of surviving, but I also don't like to be ignorant. It is important for me to be at peace with the facts of my diagnosis and fight like heck to not become one of the statistics. I see these same statements made by the other women who have started blogs. "I'll be one of those that lives to see many more of my children's birthdays" or "get past these first two years and I'm golden" or "I will be one of the few that beats it". I have yet to come across a blog with one of these optimistic statements that that author is still alive.

I have no clue how I have gone 28 years of life without experiencing extreme pain or hardship like this. I have never had a family member or close friend pass away. I've just lived my life so oblivious to all of the horrible pain that exists out there. It doesn't matter if you are a "religious" person or not- life is not fair and it is not easy. We all know we are going to die but how many of us are actually willing to talk about it, think about it, and plan for it? We are programmed as humans to fear death and try to ignore its inevitability.

I am sure by now I have lost some readers and that is okay. I am sure I will continue to lose more. Maybe because I use profanity or talk about dying or seem to be more negative than positive. That's not true- I am just being real. All of those things are going to continue. I do this to help myself and it's not fair for me to hold back anything out of fear of making someone else uncomfortable. I used to be one of those people who would roll my eyes at those that utilized a public platform like Facebook or a blog to overshare personal information. I would think of those people as sad individuals who were crying out for attention. I would never do that. Now, it was different if I saw someone post introspective thoughts about loss or pain, as though these mundane topics made their thoughts more worthy of sharing - as opposed to what they ate for breakfast or why they're pissed at their baby daddy. I scoffed at those who exposed their personal lives on social media and am eating my prideful words. I'm doing more and more of that as of late. Not mad. This is an outlet for me and if it helps you to understand my journey too, rock on. I never had a reason or a need to over share because nothing was relevant. Now that things are not-so-boring, I appreciate everyone who lets me use this platform to vent and express my thoughts and feelings. My hope is that someday there will be someone that is facing the same battle as me and is feeling as scared as I am, and they come across my posts and realize that they are not alone. My hope is that my transparency, although it may be difficult for my loved ones to read at times, will help someone else someday. Sharing thoughts and experiences creates longevity. No matter what may happen to me, these words and this page will always exist. FYI- I have not lost hope. I am more hopeful than ever and I am at peace. Let me go on record being that girl that says "I'll be the one in a million to beat this". Wishing each of you a productive short work week and another seamless chemo round for me on Wednesday. XO

Diane: *Since she was feeling better, Kevin and I grabbed Lindsay and went downtown to watch the fireworks on July 3rd. I'm sure we were all thinking about past 4th of July celebrations - hanging on the rooftop patio of Lindsay's apartment at the corner of 4th and Brady Street, the perfect location for sipping some cocktails and watching Red, White & Boom, or the BIX Road Race! That year was somewhat different, but we still had fun!*

Later in the evening on July 4th, apparently after Lindsay wrote the previous post, Kevin and I, and our dear friends, Debbie and Jerry, were determined that Lindsay would have some fun this 4th of July! Debbie and I called to tell her we were coming to get her for a nighttime splash in their pool. She was feeling better and we convinced her to grab a suit and we picked her and Lola up. It was a night to remember! Dear friends wanting to make sure she had fun. And she did!

As Lindsay writes in her last post, "My hope is that someday there will be someone that is facing the same battle as me and is feeling as scared as I am, and they come across my posts and realize that they are not alone. My hope is that my transparency, although it may be difficult for my loved ones to read at times, will help someone else someday. Sharing thoughts and experiences creates longevity. No matter what may happen to me, these words and this page will always exist."

And that, my dear readers, is why I am doing this. As hard as it has been, I owed it to Lindsay. To fulfill her hope that her words and experience will be accessible to many who loved her and those who never had the privilege of knowing her.

49

Lindsay's Post 7-6-16

Today is Wednesday, July 6th. I am just climbing into bed after a very long but great day! It started around 4 AM this morning when I was woken up by all the crazy thunderstorms. I couldn't get back to sleep. Watched TV and surfed the web for a few hours until it was time to get ready to head to the oncologist. We met with the doctor, who did a full upper body exam then talked to us about the concerns I've mentioned over my last couple posts. We also received the results from the genetic testing and...... Wait for it.... All NEGATIVE. Zero mutations found out of the 25 genes that were tested. Go figure, right!!! The good news is that my family members do not need to get tested or have any concern that they are carrying any cancerous genes- which is very relieving. The bad news is that this was one of the last pieces of information that could have potentially given us some sort of "why", considering all other tests for hormones/receptors have been negative as well. So, there is officially zero signs pointing to any sort of "cause" for my cancer. Chalk it up to BAD LUCK, they say. A freak occurrence. The one in a million. Quite frankly, I should be heading down to the new casino and testing my luck. If the cards I was dealt in life have the same odds as someone winning the lottery.... Shit anything is possible!!

Doctor was not concerned with my head cold and congestion- which was good. Feeling almost 100% today, after having a bad day yesterday. The restlessness isn't a result of the increased anxiety meds - he said that the higher dose should be doing the opposite (shutting my brain OFF, not turning it on). But I will go back to 50 mg to see if I notice a difference. Gained 4 pounds since last week after I had been steady for the couple weeks prior so the steroids are still doing damage after all. Boo. My treatment dose was increased, probably because I reached a new weight category. Again, NOT something anyone who knows something seems concerned about. Seems like it's a normal occurrence, just like the cold, so that's good, I guess. My blood counts were normal. Oh, and I am approved to travel! As long as I am not missing a treatment (has to just be a weekend thing).

My mom is taking me to go see Mariah Carey perform her top hits in Las Vegas at the end of August. Booked that trip after we left the 5 hour doctor visit. So that is definitely giving me something to look forward to next month. And finally, we spoke with the doctor about my surgery a bit. Since we found out from the genetic testing results today that I do not have the BRCA genes- the biological chances of my left breast getting the cancer is not really a concern. I had wanted the double mastectomy regardless. I didn't want to take the chance. My doctor is now suggesting that I only have the right breast removed, because having both would only increase my chance of getting an infection, and would also make the surgery itself more extensive/more time needed to recover before being able to start radiation. Although, he did say that it was ultimately my decision so I will definitely be looking into it and weighing the positive and negatives of both options. We don't need to/won't make a final decision on the surgery or discuss it further with the surgeon for a few more weeks.

As several saw on my Facebook page: my day was made the second my new BFF at chemo, Jane, strutted into the treatment room wearing her #SlaySquad shirt. She paired it with super cute flats, a crisp pair of Chicos capris, a silver chain hanging belt, a straw sun hat with pink bow, pink diamond hoop earrings and full make up (per usual). What. A. Boss. Literally the sweetest human being I've ever met. I'm not sure of her exact age but my guess would be early 80s. Her personality and style reflect that of someone half her age. She has the kindest heart. Today was the first time I've seen her and her husband Jim (also amazing) since they arrived at my benefit - right when my two friends had climbed up onto the bar to take a shot and grind to Britney Spears. They always see me at chemo reading my bible, no makeup, sweats always, just chillin. Totally didn't suspect that I was the wildest person ever- with some equally fun friends who get buck at 2 PM on a Sunday at a cancer benefit. Anyway- they jetted the party scene pretty quickly after laying their eyes on all that sinful fun happening- but Jane know whatsup. Showed up today looking like the baddest old lady in town. And I loved it. She's wild on the sneak too, or was in her day- guaranteed.

I attended my first "group session" at Gilda's Club tonight (my new treatment makes me hyper from the steroids on treatment days so instead of being exhausted every Wednesday afternoon like I was before, I get tons of energy, so I was finally able to go tonight.....tomorrow will suck tho). I am SO GLAD that I attended. I have never felt so welcomed and understood! It

51

is so hard to deal with so many things on a day to day basis when you're dealing with cancer. Nobody truly understands what you go through unless they've gone through it. I learned tonight that the dark thoughts and feelings I'm having are not unusual and that I am NOT ALONE. It's not a physical aloneness - it's mental. It's the craziest thing to understand. The dynamics between caregivers and friends…all the emotions and life changes for the patient.....not having a way to communicate effectively or feel relatable or understood at all. It also gave me insight on things that I should anticipate experiencing... Things I hadn't even thought about. I didn't think it was possible. These people are just like me. They deal with the same internal struggles that only a person that HAS cancer gets, and for the first time since my diagnosis, I felt empathy... I gave it and I received it. It was seriously so encouraging and I will definitely be attending more and more of the Gilda's Club programs... As many as possible. It will 100% be a huge part in my coping process going forward and I am so, so thankful that I made myself go tonight. I am anticipating the next two days will be spent in bed. I hope the rest of your week is much more entertaining! XO

Diane: *Lindsay fell in love with Jane and looked forward to seeing her on Wednesdays. Jane wrote a book about cancer and gave a signed copy to Lindsay, which she treasured. Jane told us that she had incurable cancer and she would be getting chemo treatments for the rest of her life, making weekly visits every Wednesday. I sure hope that she's on this earth for many more years.*

I also attended the group session for family members at Gilda's, while Lindsay was in the other room with the others dealing with their cancer diagnosis. I wasn't really able to talk, so the facilitator told everyone about my daughter. I just cried. It was this night that I decided to talk to my doctor about something to help with my sleeplessness, anxiety, sadness and overall stress. Welcome, Xanax.

Lindsay's Post 7-13-16
Today is Wednesday, July 13th - AKA the half way mark through my chemo treatments! As we speak, I'm receiving infusion #8 out of 16!! The past few days have been good. Sunday-Tuesday I did at least one "activity" outside of the house every day. The tail end of last week was spent in bed. I was still battling the never ending head cold but seem to have gotten rid of it finally. My pattern has become pretty set with my new treatment; Wednesday chemo

in the AM and feeling good from the meds in the afternoon, but experience restlessness from the steroids. Thursday AM usually feeling so so - start to get achy and more tired throughout the day. Friday I'm typically very tired and sore -basically sleep the entire day. Saturday is hit or miss but usually feeling much better than Friday. On those days, my biggest task for the day is figuring out which essential oil and bath salt combo I will use in my Jacuzzi tub. Sunday-Tuesday are my "normal" days where I'm able to get out of bed, have visitors, move around. I had a fun filled couple of days.

Sunday I got to see my niece and my friends Derek and Cassie came to visit me in the afternoon. Monday I ran a couple errands with mom and attended the benefit follow up fundraiser night at Buffalo Wild Wings. Thanks again to everyone who came - it was great to see so many friends and have a Grapefruit Traveler! Yesterday I had a doctor visit in the AM to get labs done, had lunch with Kelsey, then another friend Amy came to my house to bring me a meal for this week! OMG honey like enchiladas - soo amazing!! Thank you, Amy!!! Even though my "busy" schedule over the past couple days seems easy, and would have been just a portion of the daily activities for the old me, I was really worn out after each day.

I found out today that my kidney function looks normal from yesterday's labs, so I will continue getting the additional drug- Carboplatin- weekly with the Taxol chemo. All of my counts continue to hold strong. This is good news because if my counts are too low to get treatment, my schedule will be pushed back as far as surgery/recovery and back-to-work date in September. A change for the control freak?! NOO!!! Insert wide eyed emoji. Let's get through these next 8 weeks of infusions with ease, pleeeeeease. I miss working. I want my hair to start coming back. I want to get this surgery done with and radiation started. One of the most common questions I get is "how is the progress" or "is the chemo working?" It is difficult to know for sure what's going on inside my body. We can only judge the physical signs from the outside, but just because the tumor seems to be shrinking, we can't assume anything. We can still feel the tumor, especially around the areola it is still really hard. The redness comes and goes. My right breast is still much larger than the left. I don't think I'll get another scan to see what's going on inside this body until before my surgery? Definitely after it. My right breast

53

has had some pain in it recently - but I am hopeful that it is just the medicine in there doing its job. If only our skin was transparent.

Sleeping seems to be getting more difficult again. The hot flashes continue to be one of the worst things to deal with. I will go to sleep with the AC on 67 and a large fan blowing on me and will still wake up several times throughout the night drenched in sweat. Or like Monday at b dubs Deanna asks me mid convo "are you having a hot flash?" She could tell from the physical symptoms before I could - my face gets flush and covered in beads of sweat.

The wigs at this point are pretty much not a thing. I wear a baseball hat or a scarf almost every time that I'm leaving the house. It is just way too dang hot - screw looking cute! They said when I started chemo I would notice some difference in my skin and nails. Some people lose their fingernails or some have nails that turn black. Mine have been doing the opposite- they are growing faster than they normally do and I find myself having to file them about once a week. My hands and feet have been significantly drier though. I have small areas of skin that peel off my palms and bottom of my feet. I have had cracking on my heels so bad that they bleed sometimes in the night. Bloody and sweaty sheets in my bed - sexy!! I cannot get mani/pedis due to the chance of getting an infection which sucks. Since I cannot be in the sun, I am white as a ghost!!! Ideally, I would be spending my non-working summer days napping in a hammock or enjoying my patio and catching some rays but of course I can't do that!! Where is the silver lining here? I already have cancer dude- and to add salt to the wound I'm fat, bald, pale, no brows, no mani, busted feet, Soon will have no boobs.... Come on man!!! Throw me a frickin bone here. I thought cancer people at least got skinny?! To hell with it. No, I say all of this jokingly - I really don't care what I look like right now. I'm too busy fighting for my life. As much as it sucks, my tears aren't flowing because of all the physical changes anymore. I cried the day we shaved my head but that was the only time I remember being emotionally overwhelmed by it. I still cry myself to sleep every night - because of the situation that I'm in and the drastic, unexpected turn my life has taken over the past few months.

Looking in the mirror isn't something that I do as frequently, but not because I don't like the way I look necessarily. I am actually kind of starting to like the bald head. I get random peach fuzz and little hairs sprouting out now and then. They look blonde but could be grey. When your hair grows back after chemo, it usually comes in a different color and texture than it was before. I can't wait to see how mine comes back. I think it will be fun to go through the short hair phase, even though it may not compliment my round face. On the infrequent occurrences of me putting on some makeup or lashes, I still can look like I used to- or close. It just takes so much energy!! Ain't nobody got time for that. I know that after I beat this I can get back to looking and feeling like myself. I'll even have brand new boobies in a year or so - God willing!! Back to the fighting I go. Hot flash coming on! Life is good, God is good. Happy hump day - Have a great one!! XO

Diane: *Lindsay continued to be positive, looking toward the future, imagining a positive outcome. What she had gone through in less than three months was overwhelming to consider....and remember.*

In July 2016, writer Martha Garcia interviewed Lindsay and submitted a story to the Dispatch Argus newspaper entitled "Looking in the mirror, we can still see beauty" about Lindsay's journey to date. Martha, a cancer survivor herself, wanted to help us bring awareness to Lindsay's cancer (IBC) and hold her up as a strong and courageous young woman, staying positive and holding out hope under dire circumstances. You can still read that article online. As Lindsay would say, "Google it".

Lindsay's Post 7-20-16

Today is Wednesday, July 20th - what should have been a normal chemo day... Treatment 9 out of 16. BUT our day did not go as planned. My mom and I got to the doctor's office around 9 AM and waited patiently to see the slay master himself before my chemo infusion. A nurse accessed my port, took my vitals and blood counts as they normally do (down 3 pounds- woo hoo!) then Doc came in to do his bi-weekly exam. I had mentioned to him that I had noticed a pea sized lump on the top of the cancer breast a few days ago and another protruding red spot on the areola. I really didn't think it was anything - maybe swollen glands or some kind of normal skin reactions to the chemo. As soon as the exam started, I could tell that doctor was not his cheerful self and he took more time than usual examining. I could also feel pain on the right side of my breast as he pressed on it- a pain that was all too familiar and reminded me of how it felt before I had started my treatments.

Over the past week or so, it seems that the cancer has outsmarted the medicine. The warmth, redness and swelling, in addition to the two new lumps, were a clear sign to doctor that things had suddenly taken a turn in the wrong direction and he was concerned. It seems that the upper breast lump is potentially another tumor. He has decided to send me to the University of Iowa cancer clinic for a second opinion and has stopped my current chemo regimen. SO I did not get treatment today. The Taxol/Carboplatin recipe will be discontinued.

We will meet with the new oncologist in Iowa City this Friday afternoon and see where we go from there. At this point, it sounds like my local doctor is simply getting input from the IC specialist before making a final decision on what to switch my treatments to, which we are perfectly fine with of course. We know that the red devil worked well for the first 4 treatments but damn that was tough on my body. I knew this Taxol business seemed way too smooth! We are unsure at this time how involved this new oncologist will be with my ongoing treatment plan, whether the U of I cancer center will be a place we are frequenting, how extensive the consultation will be, whether we will be there for a few minutes or a few hours... There are still a lot of unanswered questions so for now all we can do is wait and see what Friday brings. Will update everyone on here of course as we have more information. Another bump in the road (and in the breast) - but trying to stay strong. Thanks for your continued prayers of strength for my family and I.

Diane: *Off to Iowa City we went to see the breast cancer specialists at the University of Iowa Hospitals & Clinics. Tom would meet us there. I'm sure the last thing Lindsay ever imagined happening during her college years was that she would one day return to her alma mater as a cancer patient.*

Lindsay's Post 7-22-16
Today is Friday, July 22nd. My parents and I met with an oncologist at the University of Iowa today who specializes in breast cancer. He reviewed my

history, my understanding of where we are at with the cancer/treatment, and did an exam. We also met with a breast surgeon while we were there. Since the cancer has grown, they are once again unable to feel the margins or edges of the tumor. If you recall, I think it was after my second initial chemo treatment of red devil that the doctor was able to measure the tumor at 7 cm. I had responded to that drug right away. Now we are trying to get back to the point where we can measure it again.

Late Wednesday night after I had posted, my Davenport oncologist called saying he wanted me to come in for treatment on Thursday (yesterday) AM. He wanted to give me 2 new drugs since the Taxol was not working and we were moving in the wrong direction. Navelbine and Gemzar are the names of the two new chemotherapy drugs they tried yesterday. The IC oncologist wants to see how I respond after a couple more rounds of that recipe so I'm assuming I will get chemo sometime next week but do not have that scheduled yet. If we see some shrinkage and the tumor becomes measurable again, we will bail on the chemo and go directly to surgery. That would be the best option. Of course, no surgeon wants to perform the mastectomy without knowing whether they can get rid of all the cancer and at this time it's too large. If the edges of the skin still have cancerous cells once they sew it up, it will just come back and defeat the purpose of the surgery. So fingers crossed that this mixture shrinks it and we can do the surgery sooner than later. If that does not happen and I don't respond to this recipe, they will have to come up with another plan which will probably include doubling up on the chemo + radiation - which is never good to do pre-surgery and that would not be ideal.

The doctor we met with at UIHC today also suggested doing molecular analysis of the actual cancer to look for a mutation. If anything is found, which he said was a long shot considering I'm triple negative, it may be an option down the road (if needed) for advanced therapies or studies to be used, etc. I have to go back to Iowa City on Monday afternoon to meet with the surgeon again- she's going to do another biopsy and a more comprehensive exam. Still a lot of unknowns at this point. I'm really tired after a long day and I apologize if you've messaged me and I have not

57

responded. Hopefully this post will be helpful - That is all we know for today.

Diane: *Even though it wasn't fun, or enjoyable in any way, I believe Lindsay started to look forward to the next thing. The next Dr. appointment, the daily changes, the next test....because it meant HOPE. Maybe this doctor would have the answers, maybe this treatment would help her, maybe this test would show that the treatments were working. Either way it kept her busy, keeping track and looking forward, something that was very important to her sanity.*

Lindsay's Post 7-25-16

Today is Monday, July 25th. My weekend was pretty good overall. I was still tired most of the day Saturday from my Thursday chemo plus my long day in Iowa City on Friday. I got out of bed late in the afternoon on Saturday and went to visit my niece and sister, which always puts a smile on my face. Yesterday I laid low too, in anticipation of our trip back to IC today. Driving up today, mom and I were happy to know that we wouldn't have to deal with the big hospital. We met with the surgeon at the U of I clinic located in Coralville at River Landing. Beautiful new building! It was much easier for parking and getting around- that's for sure. Before the visit, we had lunch and enjoyed some window shopping. We even stopped at Scratch cupcakes to get some goodies to take home! It was nice to get out and do a little walking... But still way too hot for me to be outside too long!!

Our appointment was at 2 and we were there until about 3:30. After meeting with a couple doctor/students, going over history, doing exams etc, the doctor did a punch biopsy of one of the new tumors- the smaller protruding one on the edge of the areola. It was a 6 mm punch. Before doing the procedure, they numbed me up and that was the worst part! I squeezed the hand of one of the students (who I thought was my mom LOL otherwise I wouldn't have squeezed so hard.. My eyes were closed!!) That sucked. But not as much as the core biopsy I had in April. I had to get 3 stitches where they removed the lump. I will get those removed in a week. It is getting more and more sore by the minute, but luckily I still have plenty of pain meds so I will be okay! After that was finished, she (yes- my new surgeon is a female and I love that) told us her thoughts on how to proceed. As she had briefly

58

mentioned Friday, she does not feel comfortable performing the surgery at this point. She would like for me to continue with this new chemo regimen for a couple more weeks to see if we notice an improvement. I will go back to see her again 2 weeks from today. She would like for the redness that is covering my breast (where the cancer is) to decrease by about 2 cm before she is comfortable doing the mastectomy. If we go back in two weeks and it has NOT improved like she'd like for it to, there will be two options for us to consider. She could stop the chemo and decide to go to surgery anyway, although it would be a much more extensive surgery, which is why she is uncomfortable with it, as she would need to take fat/skin from another area of my body in order to close the hole in my breast since she would have to remove so much of the skin that she wouldn't be able to close it naturally.

The other option would be to try and add the radiation on top of the chemo and see what happens- which I had mentioned in my last post is not ideal because the surgery would be put off longer (radiation requires time to heal before surgery can be performed). They really don't want to have to do radiation until after the surgery. So - we continue to wait and all 3 of my doctors will continue to keep an eye on me to see if/when we make a change. We will wait and see if the biopsy provides us with any new information and we will see if the redness that has returned to the breast decreases over the next 2 weeks with the new chemo. AND The coolest part of the day was finding out that I am going to be the topic of discussion for the university's tumor board meeting this Friday. A tumor board is basically a group of oncologists and surgeons who are experts in their field that get together to discuss treatment plans and share ideas about how to move forward with special cases. Also called a multidisciplinary opinion. So, it's pretty awesome that my case is going to be looked at by many of the best and smartest physicians in the country! That's something that not many people get to say that they've had - which can be a good and bad thing to know that my case is getting such special attention. It will be interesting to see if anyone gives any new input or suggestions on shifting our treatment plan at all but we were very excited to hear this news. I'm sure I will be sore tomorrow where I had the procedure today, so I am planning on taking it easy the next couple days until I have chemo again here in Davenport on Thursday AM. Thanks for the continued positive thoughts!!

Diane: Lindsay really liked Dr. Lizarraga at the U of I. They clicked right away, and Lindsay was happy to have another great doctor on her side fighting this battle.

I'm so appreciative for the expertise we received from my sister-in-law, Carol, throughout Lindsay's cancer journey. She was an oncology nurse practitioner and it seemed like every time we left a doctor appointment, we were on the phone with her asking for clarification and her perspective about what we'd just been told. Right from the beginning, Carol's feedback and knowledge meant so much to us both.

Lindsay's Post 7-28-16

Today is Thursday, July 28th. Wow- I cannot believe this month is almost over. My 12-week leave of absence from work seemed like an eternity initially, but it is already half over. With the interruptions in my treatment plan though, who knows if that return date will remain. Just trying to take it one day at a time. The anxiety medication has really been helping keep my worry and anxiousness about not working at bay.

There was yet another unexpected hiccup today when I went in to get my second dose of the new chemo recipe. My white blood cell counts were too low so I couldn't get the treatment. I have to go back tomorrow morning and they will check the counts again. If they're still too low, they may give me the Neulasta shot. That's the one that makes me feel like I got hit by a bus with all over body aches boo! If the counts are better, I will get the chemo tomorrow. It seems like every time I think we have a new "plan" something comes up. So I've decided not to plan anything anymore!! It's all good. Thank you to my kind friend Deanna and my dad for getting up early and shifting their schedules this AM to help transport me to and from my appointment. And to my brother for taking me back tomorrow. And Rachel and Kristin and Tara for offering. And my mom for normally doing it every week. I'm so lucky to have such awesome family and friends!!!

The area where I got stitches on Monday seems to be doing fine. The discomfort only lasted about a day. I have started to experience neuropathy over the past few days. Neuropathy is a nervous system disorder, usually in old people. Mine is a side effect of chemotherapy. Your hands and feet feel

60

tingly and numb. Like when you sit cross legged too long and your foot falls asleep. Except it's constant and it's only in the tips of your fingers. At least for me. They usually say it occurs in both your fingers and toes but so far I don't feel it in my toes, just my fingers. My tongue felt numb, weird this past weekend, but I didn't think much of it. That went away after about a day but I'm sure it's all related. My hands feel like I've been sitting on them for hours and they've fallen asleep but won't wake up. It's nothing unbearable, just strange and uncomfortable. I feel like a 60 year old trapped in a 28 year old's body. My fingers are about as swollen as sausages, at least that's how it feels. Fluid retention (edema) in hands, feet, face, ankles is normal with chemo also- I'm sure there's some correlation with the swollen fingers and tingling fingertips occurring around the same timeframe with the neuropathy.

I will spend the rest of today relaxing and I am hopeful that I can get my treatment tomorrow! Sounds like either way I'll have to lay low again this weekend... Which sucks cuz I wanted to enjoy Bix festivities with my friends on Saturday and had a baby shower to go to on Sunday. I can't wait to get healthy and get back to living a normal life!! For now, nap time. XO

Diane: *Always being positive, expecting that she will one day be well and healthy again. She never stopped and kept us ALL hoping.*

Lindsay's Post 8-5-16
Today is Friday, August 5th. TGIF! I have had a great few days. Have been feeling much better since Tuesday. Even enjoyed some wine yesterday. I am very glad that I had an "off week" from chemo this week. My body really needed it, especially after last weekend. Never in a million years did I think I would be so thankful to feel "normal" or able to get out of bed for more than two consecutive days. I still am dealing with back pain and cannot walk around or stand very long- but I'll take it. I had an appointment with my oncologist today as a follow up to Monday, and my WBC counts were too low again, so I wouldn't have been able to get treatment even if I wanted to.

The redness has decreased again since Monday as a result of last week's treatment. We are noticing the same pattern, that the treatment will "work" after about 4-6 days, and eventually the cancer will "bite again". This is why I am now being monitored so closely. We are tracking the improvement windows, and they will play a crucial role in my always-changing treatment plan. The chance of the breast looking better, happening at the same time as my counts being normal are slim. The window for surgery would have to be on a day that I have both happening at the same time. We know that my counts will be back up in a few days, and are hoping that the redness AKA "angry cancer" stays away through the weekend. Especially since this is the first time we have had an "off week". If we meet with the surgeons in Iowa city on Monday and things are still this way, we wouldn't be surprised if the surgery was scheduled on short notice, maybe even within a couple days, to take advantage of the window. We are very anxious to see what we find out Monday. At this point I just want to be cut open and I want that cancer out of me. Even if it means having to do an extensive surgery and use tissue from another area of my body to close it up. But the risks of doing it this early are still high and Doctor explained today that it will be difficult to get clear margins. I will post an update Monday once we see what the surgeons have decided.

We also got the results of the punch biopsy today, which surprise, surprise was still triple negative. The good news is that the new tumors that have formed in my breast are not different TYPES of cancer- it's all coming from the same tumor. If one of the receptors were to be positive, even though it would be good news because we would be able to target something, it would mean we would be dealing with two beasts rather than one. My friend Eva named my tumor "Becky (with the good hair)" today. She said we need to name this Bitch that we are going to kill. So there's that.

In other news- My hair is slowing starting to grow back I think! My bald head, if glanced at in the right light, has some fuzz! It feels thin. My doctor said my hair may start coming back with the new recipe because these aren't drugs that cause hair loss like the past 2 recipes. This means I may have to bring my razor out of retirement soon. I will admit that not having to shave my legs or anywhere else on my body has been quite lovely. One of the few perks of going through chemo! I will be getting out of the house for a bit tonight, and plan to tomorrow as well, assuming I will continue to feel up for it. I hope you have a great weekend! XO

Diane: *This would be one of Lindsay's last weekends feeling "good" and being able to do some fun stuff and feeling okay doing it. But another visit to the surgeon on Monday. Little did we know how drastically everything would change.*

Lindsay's Post 8-8-16

Today is Monday, August 8th. As most already know from Facebook, I had an awesome weekend! Having a week off from chemo was the best thing ever. I went out with friends both Friday and Saturday nights and got to feel like myself again. Lots of laughs and good times. It was so refreshing. And I'm glad I was able to take advantage of feeling good this weekend because I will only have the luxury of "being free" for a couple more days. We met with the surgeons at the University of Iowa this morning and found out that that I will be having surgery this Thursday. They won't give me an exact time until Wednesday afternoon, but it will be late morning, around 10 AM is what they're planning.

The surgery will be long, probably over 5 hours. First, the oncology surgeon will do the full right breast radical mastectomy, which will include the entire breast and all 20-30 of the axillary lymph nodes under the arm. That alone takes about 2-3 hours usually. Then the plastic surgeon will step in and perform his half, which they said could take just as long. As mentioned previously, since the tumor is still so big, this is not a conventional operation. They will not be able to close the wound on the chest naturally. The plastic surgeon will perform a latissimus dorsi flap procedure, which basically means that he will take a flap of skin/fat/muscle from my back and transfer it up front just to close the hole. I will have a large scar from the middle of my back, right under my scapula (shoulder bone) across to the large breast removal scar in front. Half my body will be a dang scar! But I don't care. The cosmetic part of all this is really the last thing on my mind right now.

So much for choosing the double mastectomy. That is not an option. I will have to be the uni-boob girl. So now I'm not just the fat bald lady with busted feet, add Uni-boob and covered in scars to the list! They told us that scheduling this big of a surgery 3 days prior is unheard of for Iowa City- if that gives you any indication on the urgency of the whole situation. Since we know my body is rejecting the chemotherapy, the best choice is to just slice me open and try to cut the thing out before it spreads to other organs. The surgeon told us that the chances of getting all the cancer with this procedure are not very high. If there are still supraclavicular nodes that are cancerous, those can't be removed during surgery. She's going to take as much as she possibly can and all we can do is hope and pray for clear margins. We will still have to do radiation after I am healed from the surgery in a few weeks, and maybe more chemo depending on how much cancer is still left in there once they're done.

I'm not sure how I'm feeling right now. Part of me is really excited just to get the tumor out of me, but it's also very rushed and a risky procedure so of course I am scared. My blood counts are still on the low end and there is high risk for infection. But I know that this is all we can do at this point and it's what needs to be done. My good friends Kristin and Tony live in Iowa city and are going to meet us Thursday morning to take Lola before we go in. They'll keep her through the weekend. Docs said I will probably be in the hospital for at least 2 nights so I'm thinking they will send me home Saturday. That of course will depend on how much they end up having to take once they open me up, how everything goes, how I'm doing, etc. We will get Lola and head home once I'm released. I cannot thank you enough Bracks! Getting her taken care of was my biggest concern and that takes a lot off my mind.

My mom will stay with me for who knows how many days to take care of me. I ordered a recliner that I will set up to sleep on next to my mom where my mom will sleep once we get back home. I will have two drains that she will empty for me- one drain in my back and one in the front. It may be hard for me to type an update using my left hand so I can't promise that I will be able to keep everyone updated as extensively as I'd like to for the next week or so, but I will ask my mom or friends to help me write something to at least keep everything in the loop with how things are going. My mom loves that she will have to wipe my butt again, just like the good old days 28 years ago. She said she was going to wheel me out to the deck and hose me down instead of wiping me if I don't stop cracking the caretaker jokes. My mom is

64

an angel- I don't think I would consent to do the surgery if I didn't have her to take care of me.

I know so many others want to know how they can help or what they can do. All you can do is pray. Please pray for the medical team at the U of I and all of the people that will be involved in my operation on Thursday, especially the two surgeons. Pray that God and angels will be in the operating room with us, guiding the surgeon's hands. Pray that we are able to get most, if not all, of the cancerous cells out of my body. Pray that the surgical team takes what they need to, but not too much. Please pray for my recovery- that I will have minimal pain and discomfort, that there are no infections in or around the incision areas, and that I'm able to rest and find peace while at the hospital. Please pray for my family- that they find strength and patience throughout the procedure. Thank you in advance for your prayers and positive thoughts. We are going to need as many as we can get. Thursday is the big day. Let's do it.

Diane: *Of course, I took care of her. She was my baby! It wasn't something anyone else could or should take on. No one could do it better. It had to be me. We were all praying very hard for a positive outcome and that the surgeon would get it all.*

Lindsay's Post 8-15-16
Today is Monday, August 15th. I am at home recovering from surgery after being in the hospital for 3 days. Last week in the days leading up to surgery I had lots of errands to run and things to get in order around the house, so those three days went by quickly. We headed up to Iowa city at 7 AM Thursday morning. We were in prep for a couple hours. They marked on my back and my front. The chunk that the plastic surgeon drew on my back was a lot larger than I had anticipated. The doctors decided to do a small procedure prior to the surgery, which they called a block. It is basically an epidural. They did an ultrasound all around my chest and armpit and found the spots to inject the block. This was supposed to help with pain on the actual breast and last for about a day. By the time I got into the operating room it was about 11:30. Next thing I knew, I was waking up in recovery around 6 PM. I was in my hospital room by about 8 PM. The surgery ended

up taking almost 7 hours. The first thing I remember about waking up in recovery is that my tongue felt really swollen and sore. I mentioned it that night a couple times but it looked normal. I woke up the next morning with a huge blister covering my tongue and getting bigger and bigger! It must have been from the intubation but it was not fun and to this day is still super swollen and sore.

Thursday night was difficult. We had to share a room and the roommate next to us decided to leave the tv on all night, text with notifications turned on full blast all night, and eat very loud snacks all night. And of course, the doctors and nurses were coming in to check on me and give me medication every couple hours so needless to say, it was a long night! The surgery itself went well. The oncology surgeon had gotten the entire breast removed with almost clear margins, except for one area on the far left near the chest bone, where she had to end up going back and taking more than planned. The lymph nodes were really fairly easy to extract - she took all of them. I asked her to take photos of the tumor and the lymph nodes after she had taken them out, because I'm a creep like that, and I'm not going to post the pictures BUT if anyone is interested let me know and I'm happy to share. Pretty awesome/unbelievable to see how massive the thing was. Then the plastic surgeon came in to do this part. The flap that he removed from my back was probably about 6-8 inches or so across and 4-5 inches high. The shape of a football. It's so weird to feel that chunk of back now in the front. There is no feeling it in. It feels much smoother to the touch than my breast/stomach skin. The whole thing is really incredible- like a work of art.

I have 3 drains that I have to keep in for 10 days. My mom has had the pleasure of draining them twice per day. The tightness in my back and armpit is the worst part as far as discomfort. I have some tightness and pressure in my chest also but the back is the worst. It gets better every day but I'm still in a lot of pain - no matter how many drugs I take. The second night in the hospital I had a fever of over 101 and had some fluid in my lungs causing shortness of breath and a super high heart rate. I have been using a breathing machine to prevent pneumonia. I'm able to take deeper breaths every day.

The fever was back down by Saturday AM. We ended up being discharged on Sunday. I am home now and am trying to get as must rest as possible. I am usually sleeping every couple hours. I really appreciate all of the flowers, cards, gifts, meals, prayers, well wishes and all the visitors that stopped back to see me Friday and Saturday while in the hospital. Your kindness has lifted my spirits and will continue to be key in my recovery. These have been the worst few days of my life. I've never experienced this much pain and discomfort. I have gotten one sponge bath and am going to attempt another bath tomorrow. My mom is staying with me and will plan to for at least the rest of the week. It's still not possible for me to get up out of my chair or do much of anything without help since my back muscles are worthless. I have follow up appointments in Iowa city next Monday with both surgeons. At that time we will get more information on the pathology reports and what they found from the removal, and where we go from here. Just taking it one day at a time still. Thank you, God for getting me through the surgery successfully and please help me to recover quickly and get good reports next week. Thank you everyone!!

Diane: *Her time in surgery was excruciating. Since Kevin had to stay home and run the GL, I was so blessed to have Tom, Mary, and my two sisters with me as we waited, together. Finally, she was out of surgery, almost seven hours later, and we received the best news - or so we thought at that time. Dr. Liz reported that she got clear margins after cutting more than they thought they needed to. I started crying, I was so relieved to hear this news! Then, everyone left me at UIHC, and I waited alone for another stressful two hours before I could see Lindsay. Our time in the hospital was not fun and Lindsay would have many painful days ahead of her. I did my best to keep everyone updated since Lindsay wasn't able to write a post for another four to five days.*

What Lindsay didn't write about, or didn't realize, was how scared I was. I know she was scared, too, but she was able to talk to me about that and I did everything in my power to assure her and stay positive for her. Me...I was so scared that something would go wrong. Scared and anxious about taking care of her post-surgery. Scared that this massive surgical procedure wasn't going to stop the devil cancer from taking her away from us. Just scared. And tired. And alone.

67

Lindsay's Post 8-18-16

Today is Thursday, August 18th- one week since the big operation. I can't believe it's already been that long. I suppose the medicine and all the sleeping I've been doing throughout the days have made it go by faster than I realized. Tuesday also marked the 4 month anniversary since my diagnosis of IBC. In only 4 months I have had: a core biopsy, countless tests and scans MRI/PET etc, port placement surgery, 3 hormone injections to induce menopause, receptor testing, genetic testing, 10 rounds of three different types of chemotherapy, a punch biopsy with stitches, at least 3 new cancerous tumors, neuropathy, an ER visit, more blood drawn and needle sticks than I thought possible, 4 oncology doctors and surgeons studying my case, multiple trips to Iowa city, 4 changes in my treatment plans, an emergency chemo bail and full right breast mastectomy with a latissimus dorsi flap and full axillary lymph node removed- causing a 7 hour surgery, 3 day hospital stay, and my body to be ripped apart- front and back. I've lost my hair, I've lost my day to day life, I've lost my breast, most of my upper chest area, and a chunk of my back. I've lost respect for a lot of people, I've gained new perspectives, and built a whole lot of stronger relationships with those who truly love me.

The first couple months were filled with anxiety, mental distress, fear and chemo side effects. The past couple months have been filled with confusion, doubt, thoughts and plans of death, and now more physical pain and helplessness than most would probably experience in a lifetime. In 4 months. It's so hard for me to wrap my brain around how much my body has been through in only a few shorts months. And to think that it's not over- it will never be over. Once I heal, I will get daily radiation for at least 6 weeks. The next steps will depend on the pathology reports we get when we go to Iowa city on Monday for our follow up appointments. I will also meet with my Davenport oncologist next Friday as a follow up to the Monday follow up.

The past few days since I posted, things have gotten a little bit better. Sleeping through the night is still the hardest part, as my back gets so sore when I'm in one spot too long. Tuesday I moved from the recliner half way through the night to the couch with two pillows under my back and head. Last night I was on the couch as well. Tonight, I'm going to attempt to lay in bed with lots of pillows to keep my neck and arms elevated. Mom and I have walkie talkies that we will use since her bed is my guest room in the basement and I will be in my own room upstairs. If I need to get up for anything, I can't just yell for her from that far. Hell, she could barely wake up when I yelled for her from 10 feet away. But she's been just as tired as me. She sets her alarm to wake me up every 4 hours in the night to give me my Dilaudid and during the day she's working from my house, taking care of all of my stuff, taking care of the dog. So, I don't blame her for being out like a light when she can be- it's just easy to poke fun. She knows how appreciative I am that she's taken care of me for the past 7 days. Love ya Kost. Oh and I almost threw her back out the other day when we attempted my first bath. Not sure why we thought plopping me down in my deep jacuzzi tub would be a good idea, considering I can't even pull myself up from the couch. Mom had to literally get in the tub and pull me up with one arm (my whole right side is dead weight). I am surprise she survived. She's like 50 pounds less than I am. Not pretty. But somehow, she got me up and out! When we tried for bath #2 today, we used a washcloth with a sink, soap and warm water. Granted, I did have to squat and bend for her to get into the undercarriage to wash up, but hey ya win some ya lose some.

We hit a milestone yesterday- bowel movement! TMI yes, but I'm freakin excited- anyone who knows what it's like to be stopped up from pain killers knows how it is. Had been waiting on that for 5 days and was pretty darn excited. The 3 drains that I have in continue to be the worst part- they're so sore. I cannot wait to get them removed Monday, even though I've heard that the removal of the drains is darn right excruciating. I feel like I'll be able to sleep much more comfortably after they're out. Oh and I am becoming ambidextrous! I have been forced to use my left hand for everything, which is sorta cool actually. My mom still has to put an adult bib on me when I'm eating because I am still perfecting the skill (spaghetti night wasn't pretty) but I feel like I have a new talent! I find myself hunched over to the right side when I'm up and moving and still am holding my right arm up as if it has a cast on it. The area on my back that was cut out had to be pulled tightly to close so the tightness is giving me bad posture. I try to be cognizant of it and even though it's painful I stretch out my arm and sit up straight as much as possible. I'm now able to press the button on the side of the recliner with my right arm which was also a small victory! I could not do that until a couple days ago.

As much as the Valium and Dilaudid help to take the edge off the pain, I'm still pretty uncomfortable, but getting a little better each day. The tongue blister is getting much better- thank goodness cuz I'm almost out of Popsicles. The breathing treatments get a little easier day by day. So folks, that's what I'm going to continue to do. Move around, ween myself off meds, do daily treatments for my arm/lungs, and just keep chugging along as best as I can. As always, thank you for your prayers of healing, and for your positive thoughts as we lead up to Monday when we find out the results of the surgery pathology and where the journey will take us next. The surgical incisions are like a big balloon design with the string in the back wrapped around the side and the balloon in the front. Or a ball and chain. Or a lollipop. Or a sperm. Love you all!

Diane: *I couldn't help but feel a strange, mixed feeling of happiness and sadness when Lindsay referred to "our" follow-up appointments, and how "we" hit the road, etc. Lindsay and I were truly in this together and I would continue to be there for her every step of the way!*

Lindsay's Post 8-22-16

Today is Monday, August 22nd. 11 days since the operation. I had a lot of visitors over the weekend and that kept me from noticing my lingering pain as much, which was nice. Thank you to everyone who has come by, or asked to, and those who have helped "babysit" me while my mom has had to work. Since the only thing I can wear right now are button or zip up shirts, and obvi I'm wanting to be in PJs 24/7, I've had to wear the grandma type Jammie's that are two piece sets with buttons down the front. Pretty embarrassing. But you all should know by now that I don't really care or have any shame so whatevs. Both pairs that I have are floral and not cute. At all. But I've kept comfy and it's easy to access the drains so it's been okay. I've slept in my bed for the past 3 nights and have stopped doing the 2x/night pain killers - so I have been sleeping through the night. I've definitely felt more rested and less irritable. I'm still needing meds as soon as I wake up though. The range of motion in my right arm continues to improve little by little. I'm able to eat (almost a full meal) with my right hand now, but it is tiring. Any time I do something with my right arm it gets sore really fast.

Today we were on the road by 8 AM to head to Iowa city for follow up appointments with both surgeons. It was a beautiful day to get out of the house! I've never noticed how uneven every road in Davenport is. Every little tiny bump was hurting my surgery areas! Once we got on the highway I took a nap but It wasn't the most comfortable day of traveling overall.

Appointment #1 was at the hospital, where we met with the plastic surgeon & co. They removed all 3 of the drains - hallelujah!!! They were getting more sore by the day it seemed like. The area where the tubes went into the wounds were scabbed over and having them permanently pinned to my ugly PJs, holding onto them when using the restroom, and having to try and avoid them while resting was just the worst. Having them pulled out hurt!!! Especially the back ones. When they pulled out the back drains I could feel them all the way across my back to my spine area. The drains were on the side of the body, which was why I wasn't expecting them to be so far in there. They had to have been like a foot long. It was a really weird feeling. They started oozing right away and the doctors covered them with gauze and tape. I'll have to continue covering them for a couple days Until they fully scab over. They also removed all of the tape/butterfly bandages from around both the back and front wounds. Now that all of these things are out, I'm able to shower! I still can't bend over or move my dominant arm much so I will probably still need help when I shower tomorrow- we'll see how that goes!!

Plastics were very happy with how I'm healing. The surgery and healing itself were a complete success. I have to go back in 3 weeks. That would put us at September 12th, which is supposed to be the day I return to work. Just in case that goes as planned, we scheduled it for the Friday before instead. Yesterday I was confident that my return date would actually be my return date. I feel like even though I would be having radiation every day, that I could still work. Well, once we got to the second appointment, I realized that might not be the case.

71

Our second appointment with the oncologist surgeon who did the initial mastectomy came next. She told us that after consulting with colleagues, the U of I team suggests that I do more chemo, along with radiation. It would be yet another recipe. The final measurement of the cancerous part of the tumor that they removed was 11 cm (a little over 4 inches) the whole chunk removed was about 7 inches. The pathology report determined that the tumor had all negative margins! Meaning the outer lining of the 11 cm lump did not have cancerous cells around it. I had mentioned in my first post-op entry that the surgeon had to go back in to remove more than she had initially taken when the in-surgery pathology report still showed a little cancer left, extending the first part of the surgery. She ended up going as far as she could in all directions without hitting the sternum, muscles, chest wall. She literally took as much out as she possibly could. And it worked! At least the removal of the tumor- and that was the good news for the day. On the other hand, out of the 31 lymph nodes removed- all 31 of them were cancerous, which is pretty unusual. Nobody was expecting all 31 to be positive, but I guess I'm not surprised. The initial, level 1, axillary removal consisted of 27 nodes. When the doctor realized they were 100% cancerous, and went back in and did a level 2 node removal - basically going as far as she literally could go, just like with the breast. She was able to get 4 more nodes - all positive. The pathology report tells us "invasive ductal carcinoma involving 31/31 lymph nodes". The reason this is alarming and concerning is because if there was that much cancer in those nodes not connected to the main tumor, chances are there are still cancerous nodes in the supraclavicular area, or anything else in that right upper region that couldn't be reached during surgery. The pathology report also explained that there is carcinoma intravascular invasion present. Which in normal terms means that there are still cancer cells floating around my body in the bloodstream. The ending comment on the pathology report states "there are scattered foci of tumor cells showing treatment effect in the main tumor and in a few nodes with hyperchromatic nuclei and plump eosinophilic cytoplasm, however, mitoses are seen in this population suggesting they are viable. It is felt therefore, that there is little to no treatment response." So, if you comprehend that (took me a lot of Googling to be able to), we can understand why they're recommending more chemotherapy. The radiation only targets specific areas- but since the cancer is also vascular, the chemo would be the only drug able to circulate in the blood stream. We already knew that I wasn't responding to the chemo treatments, at least on the big tumor, but we had high hopes of all the cancer being maintained in the tumor and that's not the case. Over 50% of IBC patients have reoccurrence in other organs. So on Friday we meet with the local oncologist and see what his final decision is on how we move forward from here. We are assuming he will take the chemo + radiation doubled up plan that U of I is suggesting, but are not sure of what the drugs will be, the schedule, etc. Friday will be another important appointment with lots of information I'm sure. Thank you everyone who has reached out to check up today. The journey continues.

Diane: *I was exhausted, my body hurt, and I was trying to keep it all together. But, my God, what my daughter had gone through in a period of four months!*

Lindsay's Post 8-26-16
Today is Friday, August 26th. This was supposed to be the day that my mom and I flew to Las Vegas for a weekend getaway. I'm pretty bummed that we had to end up cancelling due to the surgery being a month early unexpectedly... But we still have an airline credit and Vegas will always be there. We really wanted to have some fun before I had my surgery, but as we have experienced almost daily for the past few months, we cannot plan or count on anything. With this journey, we can't control what will happen or make plans because things pop up unexpectedly all the time. Other than that-It's been a long, but good week.

Tuesday and Wednesday I was pretty much drained from the big haul to Iowa city Monday. Even though I took multiple naps throughout each day, Tuesday a friend brought lunch and my aunt came to visit in the evening. Wednesday my dad picked me up on his way home from work and we stopped for a beer at Public House (if you haven't checked out their patio-you should!!), then we had dinner together at Sports Fans (my fav place-mostly for the trivia). I ran into another friend and her family there. It was so nice to get out. As tired as I was, I'm so glad I decide to!! Yesterday was Deanna's birthday and I had the pleasure of spending time with her in the afternoon!! Then I got to go to Sippis for dinner with my friends!!! Needless to say, I am feeling much better and it has been sooo amazing to be able to get out and spend time with friends and family over the past few days. I do not take any of it for granted!

Our appointment with the local oncologist today was not as informative as we had hoped, but I understand that each step we make will take time, especially when multiple doctors are involved. It sounds like we are going to move forward with the chemo + radiation combo with new drugs as UIHC suggested, but my doctor is still researching and spending necessary time making sure the choice we make is the best it can be. He mentioned also potentially doing some physical therapy in the future to help with the range of motion in my right arm. It is still very tight under my armpit and in my back.

Although it gets a little better each day, I'm still not able to use my right arm much. Next week, we will meet with the radiation oncologist- this time at Genesis. I will have been in 3 different hospitals in the past 3 weeks! #Goals. It's important that my wounds are healed enough before they can start giving me the radiation. Radiation isn't something we have talked about with the doctors very much, since the surgery came on much sooner than expected. We are assuming that I'll move forward with the daily radiation for 6 weeks- but the start date is something we are unsure of- as is the chemo.

On Monday, the tumor board will put their heads together, and we have another appointment next Friday to hopefully get some more definite information on the next steps. We have not lost hope. Even though I'm getting better every day, I still have pain- as expected. At least now I feel like it can be controlled and I can do things. I still can't drive or use my right arm much- but hey I'm up and moving and getting out and that to me is a small victory- just two weeks post op. Thanks to all my friends and family who have spent time with me, prayed for me or did anything else for me this week. I continue to feel so beyond blessed to have the #Slaysquad supporting me. So much love!! And my heart is full. Thank you for keeping my spirits up. It's because of you that I am fighting! Stay tuned for more info next week. Have a great weekend!!

Diane: *Of course, we had to cancel our trip to Vegas due to the abrupt and unexpected timing of surgery, but she was still being positive about the future and was looking forward to us taking a trip at a later date.*

It was so important to Lindsay to spend time with people she loved (besides me!) so I was happy that she was up for drinks and dinners with her dad and friends that week. Summer was dwindling down and being with loved ones out of her house was her life blood.

By this time, Lindsay was taking so much medication, I had to schedule it in my phone calendar, so we remembered when she had to take it. I look back at that calendar now, for the purpose of this book, and cannot believe how much Dilaudid and Valium she was on at that point. And to think it only increased significantly going forward – just to try and keep her comfortable.

Lindsay's Post 8-30-16
Today is Tuesday, August 30th. I had a nice weekend at home, with lots of visitors who brought the fun to me! I have not been sleeping well at all for the past few nights. The pain under my right arm has been more bothersome than ever. Even with Tylenol PM or pain meds, I find myself lying restlessly for hours, will fall asleep for maybe an hour then toss and turn and repeat. Last night around 3 AM I moved downstairs to the couch I had been sleeping on before and got a couple more hours. My sleeping had been getting better for a while there- not sure what has brought on the change but hopefully it gets better soon.

Today was a very busy day, which started with my first visit to the radiation oncologist. It was mostly a consultation. He talked about the process and the next steps. Once my surgery areas have healed a tiny bit more, hopefully by next week, I'll get a CT scan so they can "mark me" for where the radiation will hit. My friend Shari who has been through this told me that they give you little tattoos on the spots they radiate. Sure enough, they confirmed the little tattoos (size of a freckle) that they'll give me once they have the exact spots determined. More permanent "scars" to add to the collection! It would be about a week after the scan that they would start the radiation, which will be every day Mon-Fri for 6 1/2 weeks. This all sounded great until the doctor realized that I still have very limited mobility in my right arm. I have

75

to be able to lift my right arm above my head in order to receive radiation, otherwise part of my arm would be radiated and that is not what we want or need. So they immediately sent me to physical therapy this afternoon. After only about 30 min of doing certain exercises with the therapist I could tell a difference in the tightness. They sent me home with specific stretches to do multiple times a day to continue working on it, and I will go back to see the PT every day for the next week until I see the radiation doctor again on the 8th. So basically, I have 8 days to get my arm from a 30 degree angle to a 90 degree angle so I can get my arm over my head. Wish me luck!! It is mostly the area under the armpit that is causing the restriction, and of course partly from the back surgery area being so tight. If I'm not able to get my arm above my head by the 8th then the radiation plan will be pushed back.

The nurse we met with mentioned that she's never seen a patient who has gotten both chemo + radiation at the same time. We are assuming chemo will start by next week, and will know when/what the chemo plan will be when we meet with that doctor this Friday. Suddenly my days have become busy! Hopefully that will help wear me out so I can get more sleep at night. Between my radiation and physical therapy appointments we stopped at Always A Woman in Moline to talk about a prosthetic. I cannot get fitted until 6-8 weeks after surgery, but it was nice to go and check everything out. They also had some camis and other fun things that I will be able to wear sooner. With the radiation feeling like a sunburn and having it daily, they recommend padded camisoles so there isn't anything tight around the chest that could irritate it even more. It's looking like it won't be until mid to late October that I'll be able to wear a prosthetic breast. Until then, I'll keep rocking the uni boob!! I don't mind.

Today when we were sitting in the PT waiting room, I was looking out the window and noticed a man digging in the trash can. He didn't look drunk or high, his clothes looked okay, and honestly if he hadn't been looking in the trash I wouldn't think he even needed a thing. And maybe he didn't... Maybe it was a hobby or maybe he threw something away that he didn't mean to throw away. I can't judge or assume and I can hope for the best, but I am almost certain that he was homeless and looking for either food or cans, etc. As I turned away from him in an effort not to embarrass him if he noticed someone was looking, I switched my glance to the people sitting around me in the waiting room. One in a wheelchair. Two with walkers. One with full leg braces. Within the five minutes that I sat in the waiting room between filling out the same old paperwork and getting called back, between the guy in the trash and the people around me that could barely walk on their own, if at all, I felt so blessed. I know it's hard for many to understand how I can stay positive while I'm going through all of this, and honestly, I'm not always positive. If I didn't have my daily Zoloft I'm sure I would have more dark days than happy ones. I had mentioned in a previous post and in my newspaper article that my perspective on life has forever changed so much, and that is a huge reason why I can stay positive. There are little things every day that I see or read about, just like today in that waiting room, that make me say "wow, it could be worse". Now to you, you may be thinking, "Lindsay- you don't know if or how long you are going to live, you just had half your chest cut off, have completely changed physically, and you struggle daily - how could it be worse?" Well.... To me, I am fortunate to have a house to live in, food in my kitchen, clothes to wear, friends and family surrounding me... I can walk on my own, I can use the restroom on my own, I can get out of bed every day... The list goes on and on. Do me a favor and try to focus more on what you DO have rather than what you don't have. Easier said than done, but I was forced into all this and I believe part of the reason God has given me this battle is to humble me and He has done way more than that. It could ALWAYS be worse and I continue to count my blessings and be aware of the positives rather than dwell on the negatives as much as I can.

When I find myself going into the dark places I turn to my favorite scriptures. Isaiah 9:2 says, "The people who walk in darkness Will see a great light; Those who live in a dark land, The light will shine on them." And that couldn't be more true. I'm sure some people choose not to pay attention to the light that is shining on them when they are going through hard times and it's easy to focus on the big question of "why me?" But I know that I was chosen to be God's messenger and to see the world through rose colored glasses. More PT tomorrow & Thurs, the Friday AM apt with oncologist to find out what his decision is for the new chemo recipe. I am hoping it is one that does not cause hair loss because mine is growing like a weed and I'll be bummed if it falls back out but we shall see! Will post another update Friday after we have that info. Sweet dreams to all!! XO

Diane: *Lindsay worked so hard at physical therapy. She was determined to get her arm over her head in time to start radiation therapy ASAP, as recommended by the doctors.*

Her internal dialogue and empathy for others in this post really got to me. She had truly learned some valuable life lessons during this time and really hoped she could impact the thoughts and actions of those reading her posts.

Lindsay's Post 9-6-16

Today is Tuesday, September 6th. Can't believe it's already September! My days seem to come and go so quickly. The past week has been up and down-mentally, physically, emotionally. I know many had been waiting for an update on Friday. I apologize for the delay! I was so so excited and fortunate that I was able to go to Iowa city on Saturday to spend time with friends and family for the first Iowa game of the season! Of course, making that drive probably wasn't the best decision for me to make.

Rewind.... When we went in for the doctor's appointment Friday, they decided to start my new chemo THAT day. As I've learned with the past chemo infusions, the drugs they give me for side effect management intravenously at the time of infusion, tend to wear off after a day or two. I always feel fine the day of and usually most of the day after. So, I was good all day Saturday and had a great time. Same with Friday- I was so glad to be able to "help" Nicky move, even if it just meant carrying small picture frames. Sunday afternoon, followed by a morning of anxiety attacks, I started to feel the chemo- body aches, nausea, the usual. Many would say, "maybe you should have rested on Friday and Saturday"... Yeah, probably. But I've decided that if/when I'm feeling okay, I'm going to do what makes me happy and not lay in bed all day "just in case" I start feeling sick. I don't want to miss important memories, or the rare chances to feel happy. When I'm alone in my thoughts, feeling sorry for myself or having FOMO, that's when I get sad and the negative feelings escalate and snowball quickly- which I will share with you today in this post. We did not expect for the doctor to say that we were starting the new chemo Friday. We figured it would be this week, but

78

because of the holiday they were super busy this week and the doctor didn't want to wait any longer, so we did it right then and there. The infusion was about 3 hours long, after we got blood work and everything done. I will get this new infusion every 3 weeks and if all goes as planned - I would get 6 rounds. That would put the end date at the week before Christmas. This recipe is one of the "old fashioned" treatments. One that they used to use for breast cancer back in the day when chemo first became a thing. The recipe is called CMF: cyclophosphamide, methotrexate, and 5-fluorouracil. I'm still having lots of anxiety about more and more things. My thoughts have become scattered and instead of focusing my anxiety on one thing, I go from one to another and get caught up in my "chemo brain" where I don't even know what my train of thought was to begin with. It's hard to explain. Since I was off chemo for a month, I wanted to take advantage of not feeling like crap and doing "normal" things in August... But the month turned out to be mostly a blur. My last chemo before surgery was August 1st, then we find out with 3 days notice that I'm going into a major surgery. Surgery and healing = two weeks down the drain.

So, fast forward another week or so and the month of August was coming to an end. But I was still longing to take advantage of the "not on chemo" phase. And even though my surgery sites were still healing, I was finally able to get around and do things. I knew more chemo was coming and I knew that the radiation would come shortly after, and I knew that in a few weeks I'd start to be so tired that I spend most of my days in my bed. I wanted to feel normal for that small window of time before that all started again. I had been going out to dinner with friends, etc and I was trying to pack one whole Summer's worth of missed fun into this short window at the end of August. For a week or so there, I forgot I was sick. I would find myself smiling and being happy about other things. They say that you go through a lot of mental distress when dealing with something like cancer but I think I was in denial for a while- and probably still am somewhat. Part of me is convinced that I will be back to work next week like I'm supposed to be, that I will get better, and I'll look like myself again. Feel happy again. But then there are days like the one I had this past Sunday where I'm convinced none of those things will happen...

When I question why I'm alive in this body- what my purpose is - and what the purpose of living is when I'm not able to be the person that I am. The person that I never realized how much I loved until she was taken from me. The person I took for granted every day. Me. The days when I feel like I am a child who can't care for herself and the burden that I'm constantly putting on everyone around me. The days I can't look in the mirror without seeing a reflection of an old man and not a hint of femininity. The days when I can't stop the tears from rolling down my face and my eyes get so swollen that it's hard to see. I don't have them very often, but when I do have bad days, they're bad. I try to keep most of it to myself, as again, I don't want to burden others with any negativity. I know that in my posts I am usually positive and I talk about how I use prayer and my faith to get me through bad days. I mean it when I say that I feel fortunate most days and that the cancer has given me a different perspective on life. But I have to be totally transparent in the fact that there are days that I do want to give up and don't think there is any fight left in me. That is an honest and raw part of this journey. But those days pass and I move to the next with a fresh start. I struggle with feeling guilt and feeling like I should be doing more with my time, even though I know rest is what my body needs now more than ever. The fact that it takes me days of rest to prepare for one "full day" of activities makes me feel weak. Makes me feel helpless, worthless, insufficient. On the days I do go out, I hear things like "you're so strong" and "you inspire me" And sometimes I feel like I want to yell "NO I'M NOT"... I am not that strong. I will say though that I make a conscious effort to be as brave as I can be as often as I can. And for those days that I can't be, It's okay. I'm finally letting myself believe that IT. IS. OK. It's ok to not be perfect or funny or outgoing or smart or courageous or glamorous, and all those things that I wish I still could be, every single day. And I keep going.

Today has been good! This morning was my 4th day of physical therapy. I had to cancel Friday since I ended up having chemo. I have some at-home exercises and stretches that I was able to do over the weekend. I have another appointment tomorrow and then Thursday morning we go back to see if my arm is up far enough for the scan I need to get going with radiation. I am pretty confident that it will be good to go. The PT has helped significantly!!! I have also been sleeping better and am able to lay on my side almost. Friday, we go back to Iowa city for a follow up with the plastic surgeon. Between PT appointments, I'm going to spend tomorrow resting up for Thursday and Friday, as they will both be long days. I have tickets to go to the Iowa/ISU game this Saturday with friends. Since I'm not supposed to be in the sun and that one is a night game, it would be one of the only games I'd actually be able to go to! I had been hoping that chemo wouldn't get in the way of it and it doesn't look like it's going to- so I'm pretty happy about that! I am hoping the rest of the week goes well and it is so nice to have something to look forward to!

Diane: *This is her* Fight Song. *She just kept fighting, and NEVER gave up. She definitely was an inspiration to many, including me, but it was hard for her to accept hearing it from others.*

Lindsay's Post 9-10-16
Today is Saturday, September 10th. I have had a great few days. Thursday, I had my follow up appointment with the radiation doctor. It was the big reveal day, to see if my arm could raise high enough to move forward with the scan and mold for treatment. I did it! Barely. It was pretty painful for me to have to hold my arm above my head for the 20-30 minutes it took to get everything done. It is so crazy how quickly the PT helped in such a short amount of time. I will continue with my home exercises, as my range of motion still is not 100%. The CT scan with the narrow hard bed that they put you on, reminded me of when I was first diagnosed and had to get a million different types of scans. Except this time, it was more uncomfortable than ever. They get you where they want you to be (in my case- both arms above my head and my head turned all the way to the left) and once everything is lined up, they build this mold around you. It's basically an inflatable blanket almost. They would put air in and let it out until everything was perfect and the mold was "made". They also marked all over me with a green sharpie to keep track of where they will be shooting the radiation. I have 3 stickers on me that need to stay in place until my next appointment - I'm assuming that's when they will give me the tattoos to permanently mark the spots. I do not have a set appointment yet for next week but we are thinking it will be earlier in the week. At that appointment we will do a "trial run" to make sure we are all good to go, and then within the next couple

weeks we will start the daily radiation treatments. I have heard that the treatments are pretty quick and easy, but what I'm not looking forward to is the side effects. They say it feels like a bad sunburn. I am hoping it's not too unbearable, but compared to everything else I've been through, I'm sure it will be fine.

Yesterday we headed to Iowa city for my second and final follow up with the plastic surgeon at U of I hospital. Before the appointment, we stopped to visit Sarah and baby Cooper at mercy hospital and it was so great. I was so so happy to see my bestie. I had to miss both her baby shower and gender reveal parties from this dang cancer interfering so I was glad I could be there to meet him at only one day old!! He's so perfect. I got a little emotional - for many reasons. Mostly because I was so happy for my friend and proud of her. But also, because I wished it were me with the newborn and had to recall the fact that it probably never will be. Loss of my fertility is still one of the worst parts of this whole thing for me. I've dreamed of being a mommy for as long as I can remember. But for now, I can love on all the babies around me! I'm blessed with the sweetest niece and lots of friends' babies in my life... Plus my fur baby Lola who I pretend is a human most of the time. She literally sleeps on the pillow next to me at night. She wakes me up in the middle of the night to go potty, she snuggles with me, she is naughty sometimes, hey close enough.

The appointment with the surgeon literally lasted 5 minutes. He just checked all of the surgery areas and made sure everything was healing to his liking. I had a suture sticking out from my back incision that he cut off for me. It must have bled a little cuz he covered it with a bandaid. It was a little pinch but not too bad. He went around the front and back with some little pliers and picked off some little scabs and dead skin. And I taught him what Udderly Smooth lotion is!! He had never heard of it. That's what the radiation people recommend I purchase to rub on my chest once I start getting therapy and I wanted to make sure he was good with that and/or if he had any other recommendations for creams. We did not schedule another appointment with him, but I did ask about when I would be able to start talking to him about reconstruction. He reminded me that we need to take it one step at a time. I need to finish radiation, see how my skin and body reacts to it, keep doing chemo and try to get the cancer out of my body before we can talk about more surgery. So, my next appointment in Iowa city is not until November when I have my 3 month follow up with the other surgeon.

This afternoon is a GO for me to head back to Iowa city again, but this time for FUN and not appointments! Can't wait to cheer on the Hawks at Kinnick tonight!! It's cool enough outside that I think I will even be able to tolerate a wig without overheating. I can't wait. That is the one thing about fall/winter I'm looking forward to is being able to wear wigs more often without sweating profusely. I woke up feeling good and I know it's going to be an awesome day. Tomorrow we have family coming in town to see Audrey and have lunch so it should be a fun filled and exciting weekend for me overall. Hope your weekend is a good one as well. GO HAWKS!!!!

Diane: *I believe that Fall was Lindsay's favorite season of the year (as it is mine) with the leaves turning, a nip in the air, and Iowa Hawkeye football. Tom had taken Lindsay to Iowa Hawkeye football games growing up, usually around her birthday on October 5th. It was a special time for them. And that year, it meant even more.*

Lindsay's Post 9-14-16

Today is Wednesday, September 14th. My weekend went as planned and I was able to see the Hawkeyes kill the Cyclowns and spent time with family. Sunday afternoon and all day Monday I was recovering from all of the activity and my body is still a little sore from all the walking I did. Monday, I found myself at the oncologist in the afternoon, as I was having symptoms of a urinary tract infection. They wanted to check my blood counts and do a urinalysis. I was informed that one of the drugs in my new chemo infusion can cause bladder problems that can be more severe than a UTI so they tested to make sure there was no blood involved and luckily it was just a UTI and nothing worse. They gave me a 3 day dose of antibiotic to fight off the infection which I finished today.

Yesterday I was let go from my job, as I was not able to commit to 40 hours/week... which was unexpected to say the least. I was hoping to extend my leave for a few more weeks, or at least work "part time" until I finished radiation but was denied and dismissed unfortunately. So that definitely made for an interesting day!! I always have and always will believe that everything happens for a reason, so I'm super excited to see what the future has to offer for my career! Thank you to everyone that I spoke to or met with yesterday and today who have provided advice & guidance! I am available for contract work effective immediately :)

This afternoon was the simulation or "dry run" for radiation. OMG it was horrible. I've been stretching my arm still, but haven't been going to PT ever since I got the original mold done last week. I figured by today it would have gotten better, not worse. I guess the stretching they were doing for me at PT was better than what I'm doing on my own. It was so painful to have to hold my right arm up for 30 minutes today- way worse than the first time, which I didn't think was possible. I have a pretty high pain tolerance and even took a pain pill before I went in just in case. Worst 30 min ever. SO glad it's over though and that I will finally be starting my daily radiation tomorrow morning! We will start with our goal being about 28 treatments and at that point we'll evaluate if we are able to do more; if so, we would do another week. So, there is not a set "end" date - it will all depend on how my body reacts. Hoping and praying that I finally respond to something positively. I won't start noticing the burns and discomfort for a couple weeks they said. My next chemo treatment is next Thursday so I'm thinking the week after next will be when I start to notice the side effects. It was so crazy how they used green and red laser beams to get me all lined up today; it felt like I was in a spaceship. The doctor took the time to show us the images and explain the 34 page treatment plan. They will target the entire right breast where the tumor originally was, all the way to the lung, the side where my drains were placed after surgery, and the supraclavicular area all the way over to my jaw that they couldn't reach during surgery. Prayers that the radiation will be successful and that I will not experience anything too terribly horrible as far as side effects, even though they keep saying I will. I'm anxious to get radiation over with.

After radiation tomorrow, I get to spend the rest of the day having fun with friends. We are getting glammed up then going to dinner/drinks and the

Dixie Chicks concert! Friday I'll have radiation in the morning as well, and then a business call that I'm looking forward to in the afternoon!! Saturday night my cousin Emily will be singing at the Grape Life- I hope to see you all there!! It should be an awesome few days ahead. If you aren't connected to me on Facebook and are wanting information on my next fundraiser, please let me know! It will be a "bra art" event. THANK YOU again to Deanna Jensen Valliere, the Steeplegate One Hundred West team, the QC lodging association and the Convention and Visitors bureau for putting the event on. I am so grateful for all that everyone is doing for me! Thanks, as always to everyone else for the ongoing love and support! Let's do this radiation thing! XO

Diane: *Of course, no one would know from her post, but getting the news that she was being let go from her job was devastating to Lindsay. But, in her usual fashion, she had made contacts and had some leads before the day was over! Unfortunately,* **employee rights** *is a huge issue for people dealing with cancer and we talked about taking some action, but at the end of the day (literally) she was moving on. She was looking forward to the adventures of the weekend. Even in her pain and fatigue, she pushed through and made the most of every day.*

Lindsay's Post 9-20-16
Today is Tuesday, September 20th. I hope everyone had a great weekend (let's try to erase that IA game Sat). My first "real" radiation appointment was successful last Thursday, and it was so fun to have my friend Cameron do my makeup and go out to the concert with friends. We had a blast! Friday morning, I woke up stuffy but assumed it may just be allergies... and thought my throat was sore because of all the screaming at the concert... a couple doses of Benedryl and Claritin later, I realized it was not allergies and I was getting sick. Was still able to have the call I had mentioned that afternoon, which was really productive and exciting! I went to bed early that night and Saturday I spent the day in bed trying to get as much rest as possible! That night my friends came in town and we went out to dinner then enjoyed listening to Emily and Laura perform at GL.

Sunday was spent resting as well... Although I did have my brother cut my hair for me. I think it was a 3 guard that he had the clippers set on, and a ton of hair came off. The back of my head is growing like a weed, and thick! The front is coming in much slower so I wanted him to cut off the long pieces and try to keep my hair even as it grows back in. Who knows- it may fall back out in the near future. I also had him take the guard thing off so I could run it over my face. I have just as much peach fuzz around my face LOL!! I'm exaggerating but it is furry! Luckily it's blonde (some say it is grey)....we will see. We had some good laughs - it was fun. Love you brothey!!

Dad and Mary cooked me a lovely pork chop dinner Sunday night- yum! By yesterday I was feeling much better! I had radiation in the afternoon and they tatted me up!! I got three tattoos- one on the top corner of the right breast and one on each side of my body, where they are radiating me. They did the chest one first which I couldn't feel since it was on my flap. The others hurt bad!! I have 3 real tattoos on my body and it def seemed like one drop hurt way worse than I remember!! But now I do not have to worry about stickers staying on my skin so it was worth it. After radiation I got to spend time with mom and baby AJ. Am seriously loving all of the time spent with friends and family over the past couple weeks.

Today I had to go to the oncology office to get labs done in preparation for Thursday; my next chemo infusion. My blood counts looked good and the antibiotics that I was on last week seemed to have done the trick. After that I went to radiation. They were running a bit behind, so I was able to spend time with the Genesis social worker, who has been helping me with lots of things.

I noticed tonight as I was getting into the bath that I have a pretty big blister that popped up right under my incision. Once I noticed it I started investigating and came across a couple other lumps near the same area. I am assuming these are effects of the radiation, but then again they said I wouldn't notice any side effects for a couple weeks so I am not sure. I will definitely get them looked at tomorrow. The only other issue I'm having currently is pain in my low back. Before surgery I was having the same type of pain. When I ended up in the ER they actually did an x-ray and everything looked okay so I'm not too worried about it- just taking lots of Epsom salt baths, stretching and using icy hot and ibuprofen to get by.

Lots of cool PR stuff going on today too - Mom and Jenny from Komen QC were on Paula Sands Live promoting the Butterfly Brunch, the Pink Project and breast cancer awareness month. I was also asked to submit my story to the Today Show via Komen. AND the city of Bettendorf has offered to declare October as Inflammatory Breast cancer awareness month, after I shared a proclamation made by a city in Florida earlier today. It's all so exciting!! It gives me energy. We need to EDUCATE and save lives! The rest of this week will be a full one. Thursday will be the first day I'll have both chemo and radiation within hours of each other. Am hoping for no issues or reactions. I anticipate being down and out through the weekend. I'm getting worse and worse at my handwritten thank you notes. I hope everyone who continues to send me gifts and well wishes knows how much I appreciate them. Thank you! Love you all! XO

Diane: Lindsay really had fun attending the Dixie Chicks concert and music with her cousin Emily at the Grape Life. So much was happening at that point, with planning for fundraisers, media attention, events, education, radiation.

But I want to stop for a moment and reflect on the relationship between my children. The two people I love most in this world. Believe me, they had some major rough patches over the years and moments in time when I feared that they'd never get along, let alone show love for each other. It made this mama's heart hurt. Thankfully, they were on a good path to forgiveness and letting the past go when Lindsay was diagnosed with IBC. My heart just swelled as I witnessed the pure love they had for each other. There wasn't anything Nick wouldn't have done for Lindsay at this point. I believe he would have traded places with her if he could have, as I would have. Family meant more to us all now than ever before. Nick loved Lindsay so much and I think a little bit of him died with her.

Lindsay's Post 9-22-16
Today is Thursday, September 22nd. Dang. I had been having the best couple of weeks, and yesterday was one of the best days ever! But unfortunately, today didn't go as we had hoped. I was so so happy because I was offered an opportunity for part time work yesterday and woke up this AM with a big smile on my face thinking about it!! Feeling so blessed and grateful that I could feel like I have purpose again. That I could focus my

time and energy on working, something I actually really enjoy. Something that makes me feel like "me". We went into the oncology appointment at 9:30 and I had shown the doctor those lumps I mentioned in my last post, that I hoped were blisters from radiation. He measured both of them- one at 5 mm and the other at 7. One felt softer than the other. He said he is "concerned" about the harder one. You could sense the disappointment in his face. He wants to see me again next Thursday to measure them. If they've grown, we will go ahead with a biopsy. Although at this time the treatment plan probably will not change either way. I proceeded with the chemotherapy infusion and we were there until about 1:30. I experienced nausea and hot flashes throughout the day. The sweat began to show through my grey t-shirt by the time we got to the next appointment. Damn steroids!! It's so embarrassing! But it's all good.

We headed to Genesis for radiation next. The radiation doctor did an exam, and had another colleague look as well. He confirmed that he is very confident the lump(s) are cancer. He decided to add what they call a bolus to my radiation treatments. Another look of disappointment from him, followed by some tears shed on our end. Not something we were really expecting to hear today. A bolus is basically a thick sheet of rubbery plastic.. it is the texture of silicon almost. And super sticky. It is used to intensify the radiation as much as possible. So they're shooting in as much of it as they can, as deeply as they can, in hopes of zapping these new guys that are popping up. Of course, this means my burns will be worse and will appear sooner. They had to put me back in the simulator machine to sketch/line up where the bolus would be placed. Then we went ahead with radiation treatment. Doctor V and Mom were both involved with the placement in the "spaceship" room (usually nobody else is in the room except a nurse). Our doctor continues to go above and beyond for us. So that was cool. We are so lucky to have some of the best doctors taking care of me. We ended up being there until about 4. Anxiety and fear are high again. This was one of the risks the oncologist warned us about before the operation- the high chance of recurrence in the same "neighborhood". It is also pushing us to the assumption that this 4th chemo regimen is yet again unsuccessful if new tumors are growing. But we pray that's not the case and have not lost hope. We believe that this is actually a GOOD thing... meaning that it could be worse (since we are already radiating here) and we are just glad that the cancer has not settled in another organ (that we know of). Praying that the lumps do not grow over the next 7 days- another biopsy would be so painful, especially on that already irritated area. I knew that the past few weeks of "freedom" were coming to an end and we learned today that we are going to come across these shitty days again as I get further into the treatment. But I believe this too shall pass. I'm still slaying!! I will continue to focus on my new opportunity, my family, and stay as positive and hopeful as possible... smiling through it all. Positive vibes and extra prayers are appreciated!

Diane: *More chemo, more radiation, enhanced radiation, more cancer popping up. Day after day, the news wasn't good, but Lindsay stayed hopeful.*

There is something Lindsay failed to post about on her blog, but was a significant event that happened on Sunday, Sept. 25th, and I want to tell you about it. It was one of those things that will be burned into my memory and always make my heart sing when I remember. It was a beautiful day and Lindsay's friend Deanna was running in the Quad Cities Marathon. Deanna had been training for months and posting videos documenting her progress in honor of Lindsay. It was a rough road and it was HARD, but Deanna knew what Lindsay was going through was much harder and she was determined to succeed. And she did it! Lindsay wasn't feeling the best that morning following a chemo treatment on Thursday, but she had promised Deanna she would be at the finish line to cheer her on. So, clothes on, out the door, I drove her over to Moline and we stood at the finish line, waiting for Deanna. When we saw her, Lindsay cheered and called her name as loud as possible. When Deanna saw her, she veered to the left and ran into Lindsay's arms and they shared the biggest hug. I caught it all on camera. If you want a huge smile today, check out the pics and video on Lindsay's or Deanna's Facebook feed.

Lindsay's Post 9-27-16
Today is Tuesday, September 27th. I feel like I have been in the best mood ever for the past couple of days with this weather. I went out and bought colorful mums and pumpkins and spent time outside this morning. My pumpkin scented candles are lit and my windows are open. I woke up chilly this morning. The smell of the fresh, crisp autumn air and these breathtaking pink and orange sunsets are the best therapy I can ever have. It's amazing

how a season can change and bring all new feelings of happiness and peacefulness - at least for me. Unfortunately, my weekend wasn't too eventful, but that was to be expected after chemo last Thursday. Nausea, aches, fatigue.. those things came and went Saturday and Sunday and I made it through. My lower back issues continue but my nightly jacuzzi tub soaks, heating pad, icy hot and ibuprofen have helped. I ended up finding another small lump, right next to the one on the side that I mentioned Thursday. And one that feels deeper up closer to my shoulder. At this point I feel like I am hypochondriac-ish with the lumps. But doctor confirmed I'm not crazy today, he feels them too. I can't tell if the big one has gotten bigger or not. This Thursday I'll get them measured and we will see if there has been a change over the past week.

Daily radiation has been going well. Going on week two. I am not yet experiencing the burns- but can definitely feel my skin getting more tender, and a little more red each day. OMG side note- today in the waiting area at radiation these old ladies were watching RHOC and talking about all the characters and what's going on in the show and who they hate. Their commentary was PRICELESS!! Hearing someone who I'm guessing is over 70 years old saying "that gold digger! That bitch!" ... I just can't! It was the best. My spirit animals.

Today was so awesome. Like I had a really great day. Yesterday and today I started going over some work things and familiarizing myself with the new company. I ordered a desk for my "craft room" and am so excited to have an actual office in my house eventually. This whole season change, getting back into the working mood... and also eliminating negativity from my days just makes me feel good. I've made a conscious effort to distance myself from places, people, thoughts, activities that are negative or do not add to my quality of life. With the election BS you're probably wondering HOW that's possible. But honestly, it's all mental. You are the only one who can allow people to get under your skin. You control your own feelings. I just laugh at all of the nonsense and honestly feel badly for people that get SO worked up about things that they can't change. That increased blood pressure cannot be good for you. You can quote me 10 years from now when we have more data on cancer and causes... I am 100% confident that my stress level was a huge factor in me getting this disease. I could probably have eaten a few more salads, drank less alcohol, stayed out of tanning beds, and exercised more... but if that's the case then wouldn't like everyone have cancer? I know plenty of people that are way unhealthier than me! So, I've come to the following conclusion. It is the mental distress that I've put myself through my whole life. And I want those around me to try and live life with less stress. (Disclaimer: I could be wrong, but it's unlikely). My poor choices in relationships, my inability to say "no", working way too much, constantly worrying about everyone else around me and not enough about myself, holding onto anger and toxicity, Worrying about everryyyything. Harboring these anxieties and stressors that are just so irrelevant and unworthy of my energy. This circles back to the control freak thing. Needing everything to be perfect all the time and stressing if it's not. Throw some attention deficit disorder tendencies in there, too. I realize these traits can be positive and are part of the reason I am successful. But it's a catch 22.

PSA: let go of the bullshit in your life. LIFE IS TOO SHORT! Who cares if someone likes the Donald. Who gives a hoot if you get cut off in traffic or if you are one minute late to work or if your shoes don't match your purse. Save that energy for something that actually matters. I wonder if someone would have told the younger me don't sweat the small stuff, stop worrying about everything, your family is the most important thing in the world, create your own happiness, don't trust everyone so easily, get on an anxiety medication (LOL). All these things that could have changed my whole state of being, would I have even listened? Doubtful. Would I be dealing with all of this right now if I had not spent the past 28 years stressing so much? Maybe. In the same breath, would I be completely independent, living comfortably in my own home at 28 if I would have been so carefree and naive? I'll never know. And I've stopped caring about what I'll never know, because I can't change it. I am happy. Today. With cancer. Alone. I had the best day buying mums and playing with my dog and going to the hospital to get radiation. The person who almost T-boned me in the genesis parking lot didn't get an F U, middle finger up and a hard long push on my horn. I just stopped my vehicle, smiled and let them go in front of me and went on with my day. Looking forward to another good day tomorrow. XO

Diane: *I just couldn't grasp how this girl continued to be so positive and upbeat. She amazed me every day. When writing my memories for this book, I sometimes reviewed Lindsay's old Facebook posts to remind me of what else was happening during this time. If you still follow her Facebook remembrance page, I encourage you to go back, re-read her posts and see her smiling face. This is how we will remember.*

<u>Lindsay's Post 9-29-16</u>

Today is Thursday, September 29th. Two posts in one week- I'm on a roll! Thanks for all of the likes and comments on my FB selfie yesterday with the rose - that was so cool to get that rose at radiation! It's been another couple of fantastic days. This morning was the follow up appointment with my oncologist to check on the progression of the new lumps. He did not measure them, just palpated. There are now a total of 4. He said he thought the 2 original lumps have become softer which is good. I asked where we go from here. He explained that sticking needles in them to do a biopsy and/or doing another big surgery to remove them would be pointless. This cancer is aggressive and we will keep going in circles. We can't keep slicing me open every time there's a new spot. I asked if this recurrence, especially so quickly, was normal. He told me "well no- but you are not normal"... we had a good laugh. It's true though. Every part of my journey has been unique, uncommon, rare, unpredictable. Just like me. I think it's kinda cool to be one of a kind! Mom told me I've always been special. Not short bus special, just special! (no offense intended) I try to keep a smile on my face during my visits, even though the faces looking back at me from the doctors feel sad.

Dad met me for radiation this afternoon and we met with doctor there as well. He got to see the "spaceship" and the radiation process so that was cool. It was a day full of appointments. Again, nothing new to share as far as treatment. We are doing all we can with the highest amount of radiation possible. So…we continue with rad + chemo and just take it a day at a time.

Tomorrow I'm looking forward to a work meeting, followed by radiation of course and then going out to dinner. Saturday can't come soon enough! It is the Butterfly Brunch (breast cancer awareness event), it's also Iowa's homecoming, and it's the first day of breast cancer awareness month.

October always was my favorite month of the year, but this year it will be even more special to me. My mom will speak at the Butterfly Brunch about my journey and about inflammatory breast cancer. She will also be doing another segment on KWQC in a couple weeks. So the PR continues and I couldn't be happier. Please help my family and I to spread awareness of IBC, especially in the month of October. We need to educate as many people as possible on this fatal disease.

I realize that the updates I've been posting on here have mostly been about my progress, struggles, and personal journey with cancer, but it's really important to me to make sure that my readers understand my specific type of breast cancer, and why I have had this journey that is unlike others.

Inflammatory breast cancer is rare but more and more cases are popping up, especially in younger women. Sure, there are similarities between IBC and more common types of breast cancer; mastectomies, chemotherapy, radiation, hair loss, pink pink pink. These are all things that come to mind for women who have had breast cancer. But the details of the disease are many. There are invasive and non-invasive types. There are ductal and lobular types. DCIS ductal carcinoma accounts for over 1/2 of breast cancer cases and has a 98% survival rate. Tubular, lobular and infiltrating types make up about 1/3 of all cases and all have an 84-98% survival rate. Inflammatory breast cancer on the other hand, accounts for only 1-3% of all cases and has a survival rate of 32-42%. Of course these are general statistics and every case is unique depending on the person, their overall health, age, staging, etc. Inflammatory breast cancer CANNOT usually be detected by mammogram because there is no actual lump- so getting an annual mammogram does not mean you have all your bases covered. The lymph vessels become blocked and the symptoms arise on the majority, if not all four quadrants, of the breast. The cancer forms in sheets and layers, rather than clumps. Common symptoms of IBC are redness/swelling of the breast, inverted or leaking nipple, an orange peel texture in the skin, warmth and heaviness of the breast. It looks and acts like an infection, or mastitis. Please talk to your sisters, daughters, mothers, aunts, friends and even men about inflammatory breast cancer.

You, just like I did, probably think something like this could never happen to you or someone you love but it can. Men get breast cancer. Women in their twenties get breast cancer. Healthy people get breast cancer. People with no family history get breast cancer. This ugly disease does not discriminate! Remember to ALWAYS go to the doctor right away if you notice a change in your breast, even if you think it's not a big deal. IBC spreads so quickly that it can turn from stage 3 to 4 in a matter of weeks. Education & self awareness are key! Thank you for helping me spread the word. #SlayIBC #MoreThanPink #F*ckCancer

Diane: *What Lindsay didn't mention in her last post was that Komen had originally asked HER to speak at the Butterfly Brunch, not me. But something you may not know about Lindsay is that she HATED public speaking. I assured her that she'd do great, but NO, she wanted me to do it. So, I did. It was an honor and I think I did okay. It was an amazing day for our family, and Lindsay read the poem before the butterflies were released. It was captured on video and I still have that. Listening to her voice occasionally makes me feel closer to her. PLEASE keep educating in her memory. It is my biggest fear - that as the years go by people will stop talking about her, about IBC, and I don't think I could handle that.*

Lindsay's Post 10-07-16

Today is Friday, October 7th. It's been a long week since my last post. The Butterfly Brunch last Saturday was so fun and I got to spend time with my sister Rachel afterwards. The support and awareness from the event were amazing. Kudos to Komen QC on all their hard work! Monday after work I got my hair bleached and that was totally fun. Tuesday I got my makeup done then headed to Des Moines to go to the Drake concert. Wednesday was my 29th birthday- yippie! I'm so glad I was able to celebrate all weekend and the night before because on my actual birthday I was not doing well. The back pain that I've been mentioning over the past several weeks was at an all-time high. To the point where Krilly had to sit me down in the shower and take me back out. It felt like someone was stabbing me in the lower part of my back and I was almost in tears in pain. Mom insisted I call my oncologist to schedule an appointment. We had mentioned this pain before, but it had gradually gotten worse over the past week or so. I also have been dealing with some pain in my chest- only on the left side, and only when I take deep breath, cough, sneeze or laugh. If I'm just sitting there it doesn't hurt. With both of those concerns lingering, doctor wanted to see me first thing yesterday morning. After he evaluated everything, he decided to send me for a CT scan of my abdomen, pelvis and chest. That's when I had to drink that yucky grape flavored milk- barf!! The scan itself was quick. The contrast they put in through my port gave me this very strange feeling as if I were peeing my pants. It was very odd! I got some more pain meds to help with my back pain through last night. We went back to the hospital to pick up the CD of the CT scan images to bring to my doctor this morning. The results showed that there is compression deformity on the L4 vertebral body - in other words, a fracture, in my lower back. Now if I were an 80 year old patient, this could be from falling down or osteoporosis or just weak bones, but because of my age and because this is new from my last scan, we know that this is because of my cancer. We also found that there are new infected lymph nodes under my left arm (remember all the right ones were removed, and cancerous, at the time of my mastectomy). The most concerning node measures 17 mm. The scan confirmed the areas that we had suspected in the lower part of my pectoral area, under the incision line, as well. The most concerning information were the nodules found in my left lung- the largest measuring about 6 mm, and another similar sized lesion in my T5 vertebral body. To summarize; we found out today that my cancer has spread to my bones and lung. I am now stage 4, with metastatic disease. My doctor here has been communicating with my doctor at U of I and they're trying to get me approved for something called a MATCH study. The hope is to find someone with a similar mutation as me, to have something to target. IF I get into the study, there would be a 20-25% chance of finding a match, And that's only if they can identify the mutation which is a 1/3 chance. The other tricky part, if I get into the program, is that I would have to be treatment-free for 4 weeks. With the aggressiveness of my cancer, my doctor isn't comfortable doing that. There is a drug that has not been approved by the FDA that we are trying to locate. I will also be calling around to cancer centers and trying to get as many options as possible. If I'm not approved for the study, and we are unable to get our hands on a drug, the estimate is that I would only have a few more months to live. Hearing this news today was obviously very upsetting for my family and I. But I've never taken no for an answer before and I'm not starting today. Doctor has given me yet another strong pain medication to keep me comfortable. We need your prayers now more than ever. Miracles do happen. Thank you in advance.

Diane: As Lindsay's 29th birthday approached, I realized that it might be her last here on earth and I wanted her day to be fun. But I was also concerned about her being away for the weekend. Thanks to her friend Krilly (AKA Kristin Brack), Lindsay had the BEST birthday going to a Drake concert in Des Moines. I remember she was also worried about being away from home that weekend. About being sick and having to limit her fun. But Kristin took good care of her and they had the best time! Once again, she pushed through her pain and smiled.

When Lindsay and I went to the hospital to pick up her results on October 7th, they gave them to me in an unsealed envelope. The intent was to take the test results to her doctor appointment and get the results then, but we looked at each other and decided to open the envelope and read the results in the car. Having a medical background, I was able to decipher the bad news. We were both shocked, sad, in disbelief that this STUPID CANCER just kept attacking her body, no matter what the doctors did. We decided to drive over to her dad's house to break the news to him. We were devastated.

Lindsay's Post 10-10-16

Today is Monday, October 10th. I'd like to start by saying thank you so much from the bottom of my heart, to everyone who has reached out, sent gifts, sent notes, contacted my family, or had us in your thoughts over the weekend. I continue to be amazed and humbled by the outpouring of support from near and far. You all are the reason I will never give up. You give me hope and faith and I know I'm not fighting alone. Even though I'd like to personally thank each and every person with a handwritten note, it's just impossible for me to keep up anymore. Please know how grateful I am for each and every person following my story. Friday was certainly a hard day for us all. Dad had already planned a nice dinner that evening to celebrate my birthday and I did not want to cancel. It was really nice to spend time with my family- being happy. I didn't sleep well that night and thought maybe I was just subconsciously thinking about the information we had gotten that day. I tossed and turned, went from freezing cold to sweating my ass off and feeling nauseous. By about 5 AM Saturday morning I felt horrible - I took my temperature and it read 102. The oncologist on call over the weekends usually recommends going to the hospital if the temp is over 101 because that's a sign of an infection. But I figured I just had a little bug and reaaallllyyyyy didn't want to lay in a hospital bed just to get fluids when I could be laying in my own comfortable bed without clothes on, sucking down water. So, I did that. I stayed in bed and slept through most of the day, waking up every couple hours and downing a jug of H20. I was sweating so bad that my bed sheets and pillows were literally soaking wet. I felt like I was sweating that bad boy out. But I woke up Sunday and still had the chills, with a temp of 101.7. I decided if I'm gunna go to the dang ER I better go first thing before they get busy.

I got right in and spent about 5 hours there. I had been dehydrated from all of the sweating. They hooked the port up to some fluids, nausea meds, pain meds, did some x rays. My temp went down right away and bounced between 99.5-101.3. By the time I left it was right over 100 but I felt so much better. So my weekend basically sucked but hey today was much better. It started early with some work for a couple hours, and then the best thing happened. Last week when we found out about the metastasis, I had reached out to some people that I'm in different IBC support groups with. I knew that day that we needed more opinions. I was not, and still am not, accepting that this is where we give up and I die. Dammit if I'm going to leave this place, I'm gunna make sure I did everything I could on my way out. So anyway, everyone recommended that I see an IBC specialist. I had some referrals to NY, TX and IL. Not only is the IL doctor the closest, but he's the best and people have been telling me to contact him for the past 3 weeks since I had my initial recurrence. But I wanted to take my time with research, until I realized Friday that time is not on my side. I emailed him last night, assuming I probably wouldn't hear back for a few days, or weeks. I received a response first thing this morning. Mom and I are heading to Chicago tomorrow, and I have an appointment at Northwestern with him early Wednesday morning. I spent the rest of today gathering all of my files, images, everything I have from every hospital and imaging center I've been to since April to bring with me. This doctor will have access to more mutation tests, more clinical studies, trials, drugs. Of course, with travel expenses and my insurance coverage ending this month, I know the costs will continue to pile up, so I have increased my goal on this page. Thank you to everyone who has contributed, big or small. Every single penny counts and I've been able to stay on top of my bills thus far thanks to all of your generosity. Feeling blessed and hopeful. Keep those prayers coming- they are working. Can't wait to see what Wednesday brings. XO

Diane: *We were hopeful that the trip to Chicago would give us some much needed good news. We'd leave no stone unturned. Fingers crossed that by some miracle, the next Dr. C would find answers. Praying to God he had some answers.*

Lindsay's Post 10-12-16

Today is Wednesday, October 12th. It has been a looonnggg day. Mom and I left for Chicago yesterday afternoon in an effort to beat rush hour and get a good night's rest before our appointment first thing this morning. We were able to connect with my bestie Amanda for a glass of wine in the city, and enjoyed Chicago style pizza in bed watching Shark Tank. We headed over to Northwestern about 7:30 this morning. There was minimal paperwork, as I had sent everything I could before we left yesterday, as far as records and documents from the past 6 months. All my past doctors and imaging centers were very helpful with gathering so much on such short notice. Doctor came in right on time and was engaging, empathetic, personable, caring, everything we had hoped he would be and more. He was not rushed, he was concerned and you could tell he truly wanted to be there with us- I didn't feel like just another hopeful patient traveling to him in hopes of a miracle. That instant connection was really important to me. The main thing we took away with us today was hope. It will take some time to get all of these new tests done.

After our initial consult, I signed up for two different BC studies and had 10 vials of blood gathered; a couple for those studies and the rest for genetic/mutation type testing. One specifically for a liquid biopsy of the vascular disease, called the Guardant 360. Another for a Foundation test, which looks at the cancer's tissue. Our goal is to figure out the DNA of the actual tumor- so Dr. C needs to get a chunk of the breast that was taken during my surgery from U of I. It will take about 2-3 weeks to gather all of this information and have our new set plan. But the best thing that we took away with us today is knowing that there is going to be an actual plan. No

98

more guessing on treatments and just hoping for the best. After the labs were finished, we were sent to get an MRI done of the lumbar and thoracic parts of my back. Now that we know where this new metastatic disease has settled, we are going to dig deeper and take a closer look at the cancer in my spine.

Friday I was given a slow releasing morphine to add to my daily regimen, and today found out I'll have more steroids that are going to be added as well- for back inflammation. The specific drug my Dav onc had recommended us finding was taken off the table. NW doc does not think that drug would be beneficial for me. Another possibility we briefly discussed was immunotherapy. So, there are going to be a lot more options for us. We know my disease is now incurable, but we want to keep fighting for as long as we can of course. If anything, I want to provide as much information possible for research and hopefully help in making more headway with the treatment of IBC. This doctor is making that happen for us. He has given us hope. So, we are still here in Chicago, as we were unable to get everything done in one day. I have to get a final PET scan at 6:45 tomorrow morning. THANK YOU Deanna and Kevin for helping take care of my baby, and everyone else who has been flexible and understanding with my mom and my last minute schedule changes this week. For now, we are going to continue with radiation and stop with chemotherapy. We will add more radiation onto my spine. This will keep things under control until the plan is finished and all tests have been studied. Since I have not been responding to the chemo, there really is no point in continuing with it and weakening my immune system (yet)... until we find out if there is a potential genetic mutation that we haven't uncovered to target with a new regimen. NW doc and team have ordered that the PET images be processed STAT tomorrow AM so we can go over everything with them before we leave town. More to come. Thank you everyone for your prayers and positive thoughts! It was a good day.

Diane: *The couple of days that Lindsay and I spent in Chicago were a whirlwind, and we kept hoping for some good news. Even though we didn't get the news we hoped for, more wonderful memories were made. We met up with one of Lindsay's friends, drank wine, ate pizza, and walked around (a little) in downtown Chicago – one of Lindsay's favorite cities. I continued to have the feeling that it was me and Lindsay against the world, fighting this damn cancer, and we kept hitting walls.*

Lindsay's Post 10-14-16

TGIF! Today is Friday, October 14th. First off, I want you guys to know that I'm super impressed by my last post because I was so out of it that I barely remember typing it. I was soo exhausted but really wanted to get an update out since I knew friends were waiting on one. Yesterday AM when I woke up and realized I had posted I figured the whole thing would be illegible and not make any sort of sense, since I was half asleep while typing haha. Shockingly it was just fine! With that being said, I woke up yesterday morning well rested and feeling much better after such a draining day Wednesday. We had to be at Northwestern again by 6:30 AM yesterday. The PET is a longer process than other scans, not because of the pictures themselves, but the prep. You have to get an IV with glucose contract stuff that has to circulate through your body over an hour. Then you're only actually in the machine for about 20 min- the MRI was closer to an hour in the machine. I slept through both of them so it went faster than you'd think. I have been so incredibly tired ALL the time. We were done a little before 9 AM with the scan, had a quick bite in a hospital cafe, then had to meet back up with Doctor to go over the images at 9:30. All that hope I raved about during my half-awake post... it was squashed right when that appointment started. Best news: I'm not showing any cancer metastasis in my brain. Worst news: it's just about everywhere else. The tumors in my spine are larger than we initially thought. The L4 vertebra is completely consumed by cancer. There is a sizable amount of cancer found in the liver- one of the largest organs. This was the first time we found this out. Meaning it has spread to another primary organ in a matter of a week. The supraclavicular nodes are still there on the right side (couldn't get them during surgery) and they did a moon walk right on over to the other shoulder, into the majority of the lymph nodes on the left side. The whole left armpit lit up like a Christmas tree on the PET. There is more lung activity than we realized, with some fluid involved on the right side. We noticed the nodules in the left lung but the PET showed pleural and/or thickening of the right lung base as well. There are multiple hepatic metastases (liver) lesions that are new and in both the left and right portions of the organ. The spleen has been working overtime because of the activity in the liver, wearing itself out quickly. The bone scan shows multiple Metastatic lesions throughout the bony skeleton. With the most obvious being in the spine, and additional spots identified throughout the pelvis, hips, and down through the femur. The upper/mid sternum and the left second rib are also cancerous. This BITCH is relentless. She's unstoppable and she's on a mission to make her way through my whole body- fast.

After going over the PET, and identifying the extent of this thing's progression, doctor decided we do need to go ahead with a different approach at chemotherapy, and right away. We had to get some poison in my bloodstream to try and stop the spreading- at least until we get the mutation test results back in a couple weeks and at that time, may make a new plan. The most important thing right now is to slow down the progression. So, they gave me a mixture of two drugs today, Cisplatin & Taxotere. They gave me a hearty dose- 9 hours worth. We were there from about 6:45 this morning until about 4 this afternoon. The good news is I got to see four of my best friends! Tara stopped by first thing to see us this morning which was the best surprise!! Krilly came from Iowa city to bring me lunch, Rachie came and sat with me for the majority of the afternoon, then Emily came by my house once we got home this evening.

Mom has moved back in, at least for the next couple days, to take care of me. They're anticipating that I will get pretty sick from the intensity of the chemo this time. A main concern is also the kidney function and hydration. I will go back in tomorrow morning to get some IV fluids and will get a Neulasta injection. Sunday probably as well. Just hoping to get through the weekend. Monday morning I will get a new simulation done for radiation. We are going to stop doing radiation to the chest wall and switch to my spine. At this point it's more about keeping me comfortable and eliminating as much pain as possible. Radiation to my bones will cause instant relief, whereas continuing with the chest wall will only cause more burns and irritation.

I am looking forward to another benefit next Friday the 21st (Bras for a Cause) from 4-7 at One Hundred West. There's still time to enter your bra art!!!! I hope you enjoy your weekend!

Diane: *It was a crazy few days and by Thursday afternoon, we were home, exhausted and disappointed with the results of the Chicago trip. Of course, I had to go work at the Grape Life when I could, but as always, getting help with shifts from our part-timers, friends and Nick. Saturday morning, we hosted a bridal shower and we had live music both Friday and Saturday nights. Every day I have together with Lindsay, I feel blessed, but on Sunday, I felt especially blessed. After a day and a half of dealing with Friday's chemo side effects, my warrior daughter slept most of Sunday fighting off the fatigue, pain and dehydration from her nine-hour treatment two days previously.*

She got up and came to me early this evening, insisting that I get into her Jacuzzi tub, filled with Epsom Salts and scents that she had prepared for me. FIRST, a facial. Then into the "spa" she had created, including a glass of wine and flickering candles. Her instruction: Mom, you are to stay in here for 10 minutes and don't think about anything. She is fighting for her life and she is thinking about me. How did I get this lucky? Lindsay was truly one of the most generous, caring, thoughtful people I knew. That day, my blessings were abundant.

Lindsay's Post 10/17/16

Today is Monday, October 17th. Saturday morning started at the doctor's office for me- Tara hung out with me for the couple of hours that I had to get some fluid IVs and the Neulasta shot. The purpose was to prevent any kidney issues and dehydration before the pain and nausea kicked in. I still felt okay at that point. Okay enough to think it was a good idea to get a ribbon carved into my head and colored pink! We left the doctor's office around 11 Saturday morning, were at the barber by 11:30 and at HOH getting the color by 1. I really wanted to do something fun with this tiny bit of hair, on top of the bleaching, as it should be falling out here in the next couple weeks again from the new chemo.

By the time I got home that afternoon around 2, I had started to hit a wall. I went straight to bed and spent the rest of the afternoon there. The Beasons were kind enough to bring over some yummy Biaggis for my mom and I to have for dinner that night. Thank you guys! I was able to have a few bites but the nausea had increased by that point. We were given a new nausea drug to try and it did help a bit. Yesterday wasn't good at all. We went back in for fluids yet again and it was probably one of those days that is harder for my mom than me- having to see me looking like death. I felt like I would vomit every few minutes. The fluids did help take the edge off. Both days over the weekend the slay master himself was in the office keeping an eye on me as well. I am blown away by the work ethic of oncology nurses and doctors. They don't get days off and it is admirable.

Stopped at Walgreens on the way home to pick up yet more drugs. My dresser is about full with prescription bottles now. My mom had to get some work done, as she has been spending most of her time taking care of me over the past week since our journey to Northwestern. I'm sure it was nice for her that I spent almost the entire afternoon yesterday asleep. My brother came over and put together a desk that I had gotten a couple of weeks ago for my new home office. I'm not sure how much use I will get out of it, but knowing it's there is comforting to me. Thank you Nicky I love you. Kevin came by to check on us, too. This morning I woke up still not feeling well, but had to be at the radiation doctor by 8:30. They are getting the simulation going for my new treatment. My breast radiation has officially stopped, and I will have 10 doses of radiation to my spine- both Thoracic and Lumbar.

Over the past few days the skin on my chest where it had been getting radiation has completely started opening up. Open wounds, torn skin, rashes, very sore. The simulation stuff should be ready to go within the next couple days and I will start the 10 spine doses sometime later this week. While they ran some tests for that this morning, we had to pop over to the other doctor's office to see if I needed more fluids and how the kidney function looked. I also have a new pain under my left breast, which is internal and probably other rib involvement. I've been having the bowel issues again with the new morphine and higher Dilaudid doses they've given me over the past week. We've tried all of the regular treatments without much movement so now we have to do some at home injections. I keep joking with mom that she is probably looking forward to shooting me up lol just kidding. We ended up being in doctor's appointments until about Noon and by that time I was ready for a nap!! I was able to work for a bit after that.

Tomorrow I have to take Lola to the vet- this pup momma has been too caught up in her own doctor's appointments that she has pushed her little girl's annual shots off. She also needs a haircut. It is her 2nd birthday!

Someone has generously offered to clean my house tomorrow AM so I plan to get some work done during that time as well, then tomorrow night is the Proclamation that the City of Bettendorf is giving; They are making October officially the month of Inflammatory Breast Cancer awareness! Thank you, Scott Naumann for your help with this. All are welcome at Bettendorf City Hall tomorrow night at 7 PM to hear the proclamation! Should be cool. Then the benefit this Friday. Please message me for any additional information on these events. I hope to be able to attend both if I am feeling up for it. Time for some R&R now. XO

Diane: *The offer of the house cleaning service by Laura Walker was so appreciated. With all we had going on and the exhaustion I was experiencing, it was just too much to add in house cleaning! Lindsay loved her visits from friends and felt guilty about delaying Lola's vet visit and grooming. So many feelings and thoughts, pain and discomfort. She was a trooper.*

Lindsay's Post 10/20/16
Today is Thursday, October 20th. I have not had the best week so far (physically) although I'm smiling mentally. Thank you to everyone who joined us at Bettendorf City Hall on Tuesday night when the mayor proclaimed October as the month of inflammatory breast cancer awareness. I was (barely) able to attend, as Tuesday was not a good day for me at all. Because of the stomach issues that are caused by the intense pain meds, I've been trying not to take them as much. I'd rather be in pain than not be able to eat or go to the bathroom. My whole body was in pain both yesterday and Tuesday and I was not able to do much more than sleep. I got out of bed a couple of times when mom would try and get me to eat something. It was really cool to see our *Everyday Hero* segment on KWQC last night- two days filled with lots of awareness on IBC.

On top of all the bone pain, I'm also experiencing some horrible skin wounds from radiation. My right neck and chest are raw with open wounds.

The creams make it sting worse and also it seems like the moisture irritates more than soothes. Am going to try to find some powder- someone had suggested Gold Bond powder to put on top of the cream. I can barely move my neck. I've also got a bad rash on my left arm from where some adhesive was from an IV last week. My skin as a whole has become so sensitive. Where there isn't bone pain, there is skin pain. It's like when you have the chicken pox and you want to scratch because the scratching feels relieving in that moment but then you regret scratching when your skin is raw a few minutes later. I find myself subconsciously scratching in my sleep- waking up to more wounds. The pain in my left rib cage continues to hurt more and more. The throbbing pain from my low back has migrated to mid back. My whole upper body is basically one huge pain. I have never been one to be able to spend the day in bed and then sleep through the night. Even when sick. If I get too much sleep, it usually just catches up with me later and I'm wide awake. Not this week. I've been sleeping for 2 days with only short periods of being awake- and am still tired! My body is just begging for rest.

I woke up this morning feeling better than yesterday. I was able to get up to let Lola out and get some water with minimal issues. Was looking forward to a couple of work meetings ahead of me. Of course, that was thrown off track quickly. By about 9 AM I received a call from Genesis saying that my new radiation treatment plan had been completed and that I had to come in this afternoon to get started. My pain has increased again over the past couple of hours- just trying to rest now so I can get through radiation this afternoon. Am looking forward to also seeing Tim and Deanna when they come by later today.

Tomorrow morning I will go in early to receive some fluids and see my doctor, hoping that will help me to make it through the day so I'm able to attend my benefit. Thank you everyone for everything you do to support my family and I. It really helps make bad days easier.

Diane: *October 18th, another day/evening that Lindsay wasn't feeling the best but got herself up and we went down to the Bettendorf City Hall for the reading of the Mayor's proclamation that October 2016 would be designated as Inflammatory Breast Cancer Awareness Month. I spoke again on behalf of*

Lindsay and the family. It was so heartwarming to see so many family and friends show up. The Council Chamber was full of love for Lindsay. I think the Mayor even had a tear in his eye when he was reading the proclamation. Here is what the proclamation said:

Office of the Mayor Proclamation

WHEREAS, inflammatory breast cancer (IBC) is a rare but very aggressive type of breast cancer in which the cancer cells block the lymph vessels in the skin and breast; and

WHEREAS, individuals with IBC risk being misdiagnosed because they may experience symptoms which are similar to those of the benign breast infection mastitis, and delay of appropriate care often means a stage IV diagnosis; and

WHEREAS, although IBC accounts for only one to five percent of all breast cancer cases, it has a faster doubling time than that of other breast cancers; moreover, the lack of expertise about IBC in the medical community and the cancer's resistance to treatment with standard chemotherapy drugs make the five-year median survival rate for IBC approximately 40 percent; and

WHEREAS, increasing public understanding of IBC is the first step toward fighting this devastating disease, and participating in Inflammatory Breast Cancer Awareness Month is one effective way to support that effort; and

WHEREAS, Inflammatory Breast Cancer Awareness Month encourages all individuals to discuss IBC with their healthcare provider.

NOW, **THEREFORE,** I, Robert Gallagher, Mayor of the City of Bettendorf, Iowa do hereby proclaim the month of October 2016 as:

INFLAMMATORY BREAST CANCER AWARENESS MONTH

in our community and encourage all individuals to learn their risk and to speak to their healthcare provider about screening for IBC.

DATED this 18th day of October, 2016.
Mayor Robert S. Gallagher

Diane: *Earlier in the week, KWQC-TV 6 had interviewed me at my home for a series they were running for Breast Cancer Awareness Month called* Everyday Heroes. *Our segment aired on October 19th and was just one more opportunity to educate about IBC. When I Googled it for this writing in order to refresh my memories, I found that it not only aired in the Quad Cities, but also on other NBC affiliate networks, including Atlanta, Georgia! I hadn't realized, until just now, the reach of Lindsay and her story. Google it if you want to see it.*

On Friday, October 21st, Lindsay's friends from the hotel and travel industry were going to host a HUGE fundraiser, called Bras for Lindsay's Cause. *Prior to the event, Martha Garcia submitted another article about Lindsay and the fundraiser. As Deanna was quoted in the article, Lindsay said she just wanted to have a party and a good time. Given the recent news about her cancer spreading, Lindsay told her friend "Don't be sad for me. All I want is to have great memories and good laughs. God will know when it is my time."*

Lindsay's Post 10/25/16

Today is Tuesday, October 25th. Since my last update, I have been feeling much better. Thursday, I received the first radiation treatment on my spine. Originally, we thought there would be 10 rounds, but found out that there will be 20. I am in a different machine than I was when I was getting chest radiation. This machine is called tomography and it's more like a CT machine- circular tube that I go into. The radiation is given from 360 degrees, so even though my spine is targeted, I will notice side effects with organs in the front, especially my stomach (yay... more stomach issues... ugh). The good news is that I should start to notice pain relief in my back soon.

Today was my 4th treatment and usually after 5 or 6 they said I would notice the pain starting to lessen. I am still dealing with the radiation wounds from when they were zapping my chest/neck. They are starting to get better and I am almost able to turn my head to the side without my skin splitting open! Thank you so much to everyone who sent creams, gels, soaks, and ideas about treating the burns after I posted last week. They are starting to scab over which is much more tolerable than the open wounds.

Friday I spent the morning at the doctor's office getting some fluids pumped in me for a long day ahead and am so glad I did. Mom and I got our makeup done after that and then went to the benefit. I won't beat a dead horse but THANK YOU again to everyone who came to the party and everyone who helped put it together, especially Deanna. It was so fun and I used the money that was raised to pay off some outstanding bills that had been sitting on my dresser. The relief of being able to do that was so amazing. I continue to question what I did to deserve such wonderful people around me. I really truly appreciate every single thing everyone has done for my family and me. Literally the day after this benefit, my friend Jackie told me she's going to do a THIRD one. Stay tuned for more information on Trivia Night coming after the first of the year! Woo!!

Needless to say, by the end of the party Friday I was exhausted and did not feel the best Saturday morning, so I stayed in bed and got some rest until my friends came in town to take me to lunch later in the afternoon. The rest of the day was spent sleeping. Sunday my sweet friends put together a little girl's day- we watched a movie, played games, had snacks, and just enjoyed time together. It was the best! Yesterday while Laura cleaned my house, I spent time getting some work done until radiation.

This morning we had an apt with Dr. C which was pretty quick and easy. I've reached the point in my chemo cycle where my blood counts are supposed to drop, but mine looked like they were still hanging on which is great. I took a nap before having to head to radiation this afternoon, then had the pleasure of a quick visit from Deanna. I am definitely feeling much better this week than last physically. I often mention the mental struggles that my disease has caused, or enhanced, for me over the past few months. I have realized, now that I'm on daily anxiety medication, that some of the thoughts I have are just part of who I am and are not going to go away. The OCD, type A, always overthinking, has certainly been controlled by medication. For that I'm grateful. But some things can't be. For example, as much as everyone tells me that this is my time to "be selfish" and only focus on myself and getting healthy, I can't help but feel sad when I find myself doing that. I don't feel like I deserve all of the gifts, cards, visits, kind words, and overall outpouring of love and support that just doesn't stop. I used to be the type of friend that would never miss a birthday or special occasion, and would constantly think of ways to give my friends small gifts or thoughtful gestures to make them happy or show them that I appreciate them. I find myself not keeping up with those things anymore. At the beginning of my diagnosis, I was hand writing thank you cards to each person that was kind to me or sent me something. I got weaker, more tired and the love kept coming in but I couldn't keep up anymore. I still made sure to send a message of gratitude, whether via social media or a text or call. But to me that's not the same. I am working on trying to deal with this and get better at making sure everyone around me knows that I love them again. I know I say this all the time but I hope all of you, especially my family and best friends, know that I love and appreciate you now more than ever, even if I forget to show it all the time.

So that's my internal struggle for the day. I'm still breathing so I have nothing to complain about- just sharing thoughts. Life is good. This weekend I'm looking forward to attending a Halloween ball with my friends and we are dressing as the Sanderson Sisters from Hocus Pocus. Fingers crossed that the rest of the week goes well and that I'm able to enjoy that on Saturday. Next week it will be time for chemo again so I definitely am hoping to enjoy as many feel good days as I can between now and then. XO

Diane: *So many people donated, attended, and poured their love on Lindsay at the Bras fundraiser. My brother-in-law, (Lindsay's uncle) Brent, and, cousin Emily, ran an amazing Bra Art live auction and the Steeplegate Inn provided themed drinks and snacks for the event. Her friend, Tim Heim, came from Arizona, a few of my high school friends that had never met Lindsay came from Iowa City, and even my aging parents attended. Although she was nauseous and in pain, she smiled and posed for pictures, allowing those who loved her to give her a hug, even though she was at high risk for infections. It felt to me like everyone just wanted to touch her, hug her, kiss her before she was gone. Even though she needed to take several breaks in the complimentary hotel room provided to her, the evening meant so much to Lindsay and our entire family.*

After the event, on the way to take Lindsay home, we realized we hadn't had a chance to eat all evening, so we swung through Taco Bell to get something for her. After all the giving we'd received that evening, we were inspired to hand a pretty pink rose from the event to the lady at the Taco Bell drive-through. It made all three of us smile some more.

There were so many things happening and Lindsay was doing her best to rest when she should, stay hydrated AND spend precious time with her family and friends. The cards and well wishes she received continued to keep her going and made her so happy.

<u>Lindsay's Post 10/30/16</u>
Today is Sunday, October 30th. Even though my back pain is still present, I do feel like it is getting better now that I've had 7 spine radiation treatments. Or is it that I am just so used to it that it doesn't seem as bad as it was before? Or maybe the 12 hour slow release morphine pills that I take twice a day have made it seem better. I'm not sure, but all I know is that I can get up from my bed and out of the car without wanting to scream and that's a big improvement from a week ago. My chest radiation burns are much better- the scabs that had formed last week over the open wounds have healed and it is just dry, peeling skin around those areas now. Almost all better. The past week has really been pretty good overall. I have definitely noticed the fatigue side effect hitting me harder now that I've been in radiation so long. It is difficult to get through a day without a nap or two and I find myself getting drained easily. But trust me, feeling tired is a good side effect compared to most of the others so I'll take it.

I was able to go to the Halloween party last night and had an awesome time dancing the night away with friends. Ok- maybe I was only able to dance a little bit, but still. Just being able to attend was so amazing! Before I left yesterday, I was able to spend time having lunch with my dad and Mary, Nick and Tara, and my aunt and uncle! And the Bebe!! My cousin is on the dance team at Ambrose and I was able to see her perform a little bit before the game started. The whole team had pink bows in their hair for breast cancer awareness and I got a pic with them- it was pretty cool. I love my family!! Any time spent together is special to me. I have spent this afternoon resting and had to miss a party mom was having at the store but she knows how mentally drained I was and it's hard for me to have to put on a smiling face and make small talk with people when I'm rested, let alone physically tired. It's gotten to the point that I don't feel like I can go out in public without being mentally prepared to talk to people. It seems like everywhere I go someone knows me or has seen my photos and heard my story. People that I don't even know. My chemo brain makes it difficult to have a regular conversation sometimes, it is another draining activity that takes effort. Don't get me wrong, my purpose with this blog and all of the PR we've done is to spread awareness of IBC so I'm certainly thrilled that so many people have heard of my story. But the attention can be overwhelming believe it or not. Even though I am outgoing, confident, chatty and you'd never think it- I'm actually a closet introvert and really enjoy being by myself. Being around people can make me feel worse at times.

In other news - My hair is finally starting to fall out again. It was ironic because on my way home this morning I thought to myself... "ok it's been over two weeks since chemo, last time it fell out after like a week and a half... maybe it's not going to fall out? Cool." Then as soon as I get home and lay down, I have an itch on the side of my head which was a little bit tender. I look at my hand, knowing what I was going to see, and there they were.. a bunch of little hairs. So it has officially begun. Just when I finally had a hairline and was digging my short hair. I was even combing it over to the side and "styling" it. It was growing back so fast. It will be interesting to see if the process is the same this time or what the differences are. Last time the hair came out in patches, mostly in the back first then on the sides. When it came back in, the back came in the fastest and thickest and the front was the last to come in. It was only a few days, a little less than a week, from when it started falling out last time to when I was completely bald. So, say goodbye to the blonde hair and the pink ribbon shaved in back. I'll be back to a chrome dome shortly!!

This Thursday is my second round of the 9 hour long chemo treatment. Hopefully it will go quicker this time. Wednesday I get labs to make sure I'm good to go. So, it will be a short week, but I've got lots to do within the next couple of days before I'm down for the count again for a week or so. I can't believe there is only one day left in the month. Thank you to everyone who supported PINK and breast cancer awareness month in any way. Don't forget to get your annual mammograms ladies. Men can get breast cancer as well. We all need to make sure we are paying attention to our bodies and get a doctor's opinion right away if you notice a change, even if you don't think it's a big deal. Have a relaxing Sunday evening. Happy Halloween!

Diane: *I cannot believe she thought she was up for that Halloween party in Cedar Rapids, but there was no keeping her down, folks. I wanted her to have as much fun as possible but knew that what comes after would be difficult. But she needed to live her life without regret. And I needed to let her. Even in her pain and fatigue, she pushed through and made the most of every day.*

Lindsay's Post 11/04/16

Today is Friday, November 4th. I guess I spoke too soon last Sunday when I mentioned my back pain was getting better because I woke up Monday in excruciating pain again. I was able to lay in bed and get some work done until radiation at 3 that day but that was about the extent of my activity. Tuesday I was looking forward to supporting Rachel and all her hard work with the AHA Go Red luncheon. I tried to get up and start getting ready but it wasn't happening. Mom came over and helped take care of me. By about 10 AM I was not well at all. In addition to the back pain, I felt nauseous and had a horrible headache. After lots of meds, fluids, icy hot, a heating pad, nap and a movie I started feeling a little better and was able to go to radiation at 3.

Wednesday was a little bit better except I vomited unexpectedly in the shower, which was random. Luckily it was just clear liquid. TMI? I think my readers are used to my vulgarity by now. We went in to get my labs drawn that morning and they had trouble getting a blood return from my port. They tried to turn the one inch needle around inside of me and reposition it but it wouldn't work. I've been having some trouble with my port now for a few weeks. I guess things build up around the port because your body tries to build a shield around the foreign object or something... so they can still push things in, just aren't able to draw out. After I couldn't take the digging anymore, they tried to find a vein in my arm but couldn't.. so they had to end up putting the needle in the top of my hand which sucks. Fun morning, huh?!

The hair has been continuing to fall out in clumps but is not as noticeable yet as it was the first time around. I guess I didn't realize how thick my regrown hair was.. there's so much coming out, but still doesn't have the balding looking yet. I definitely had a much thicker and curlier texture of hair when it grew back the first time. It's interesting to take note of all of the changes my body is going through with each new treatment.

Yesterday was a very long day. Went in to Genesis for radiation at 8 AM and met with doctor, then had to be over to the oncology office to get chemo by 9:30. We were there getting chemo until about 5:30 PM. Hey, 8 hours is better than 9! I had some visitors throughout the day, I got Panera delivered for lunch, and got a lot of work done. I've been setting up an electronic filing system and did not realize how long it would take! A project I've been working on for a couple weeks now. But it's been really nice that I can do it all from my laptop. So overall it wasn't too bad of a day. It went quickly. I was feeling okay last night but was sweating profusely... like dripping sweat from my head constantly. I was definitely ready for bed early. I woke up about 1 AM and my clothes and sheets were absolutely soaked. But I was freezing cold. Random uncomfortable side effects.

In addition to the busy day I had physically, I also had a lot on my mind yesterday. My grandma had surgery on her carotid artery so she was consuming my thoughts all morning. Dad came to visit me at chemo around noon and let me know that she had made it out of surgery fine so that was a relief. He was heading to Dubuque to spend time with them but stopped to see me on his way out. I was very happy to see my daddy!!! It had been a few days and that's too long for me. Kevin had also been having some health issues and mom had to leave chemo in the afternoon to take him to the doctor. Ugh- It hasn't been the best year for our family overall health-wise.. to say the least! I think it's safe to say that we are all ready for 2016 to come to an end!!!! And I thought 2015 was bad. This has been the worst year of my life. I woke up this morning with my back actually feeling pretty good. I did have some nausea and a headache but now that I've been getting fluids for the past hour I'm already feeling a little better. We came back to the doctor's office at 8:30 this morning to get some more steroids and fluids. We will come back yet again tomorrow morning as well for more.

I am hoping to go to my niece and nephew's joint bday party tomorrow afternoon, and I also hope to stop by my friends Hawkeye party for the game tomorrow night. And I'm REALLY hoping that I am feeling okay on Sunday because my mom and I have tickets to see Wicked the Broadway musical in Peoria. We are really looking forward to that and I will be bummed if we can't make it. If this round of chemo is anything like the last, I probably will be down most of next week as well. My next chemo is the day before Thanksgiving... I have a feeling the holidays will not be as joyful for me this year but I will keep staying hopeful. I'm just itching to get my Christmas tree up already. I hope everyone has a great weekend. Thank you for your ongoing prayers and happy thoughts! XO

Diane: *Ever since we had to cancel our Vegas trip to see Mariah Carey in concert, Lindsay had been talking about another trip, in between treatments and when she felt up to it. Unfortunately, that would require a last-minute decision and a TON of effort to get everything arranged. Many people had come to me and asked what they could do/offer to make Lindsay's end-of-life enjoyable. I even had one friend, with a LOT of connections, ask me what Lindsay would want if she could have <u>anything</u>. I honestly found that difficult to answer as she was putting all her attention and energy toward those she loved during that time. I said that if they could make a Luke Bryan appearance happen, that would be great! As it turned out, we decided to go to Peoria to see the Broadway musical Wicked. I hoped she would be up to it!*

Lindsay's Post 11/08/16

Today is Tuesday, November 8th. Election Day 2016. I'll start by saying that this post isn't going to be a distraction from the negativity that you're seeing all over social media today. It's going to fit right on in. If you're looking for a happy post, one of encouragement and hope, you're looking in the wrong place today. I wanted to make it a happy one. Something to brighten everyone's day and get your minds off of the chaos for a few minutes but I can't muster up the excitement, it's just not there guys. I will say that I had a great weekend. Got fluids and steroids as planned Friday and Saturday, was able to go to the kid's party for a bit Saturday, and enjoyed a wonderful trip to Peoria Sunday. Thanks again to everyone who pitched in to make our Wicked package amazing. It was a nice weekend.

Things started going downhill yesterday, and then today I almost passed out and puked simultaneously at the doctor's office when getting blood drawn. Didn't want to fiddle with the port and couldn't find an arm vein so back in my hand the needle went. I was supposed to go in yesterday afternoon to get my labs, but was not able to make it because I couldn't get out of bed. The past couple of days have been pretty horrible. A lot of times I feel like shit but I just put on a brave face, take some more meds and smile. Actually, almost every day. Some more effort is needed than others. I tried to do that starting on Sunday night when the nausea really starting setting in again. Part of our generous package was a delicious meal at a fine dining restaurant, anything our hearts desired. Steaks, lobster, bottles of wine, dessert, anything. I was able to have half of my side salad and a couple bites of cheese tortellini. Oh, and I'm supposed to be going towards bland options for digestive support. If this were normal Lindsay, you better believe I'd still be getting the side salad, with bread, the filet mignon, side of lobster mac n cheese and a bottle of Pinot. I wished I could have. It's instances like these where I can't hide my disease. I tried to eat as much as I could but forcing yourself to vomit in a fine dining atmosphere probably isn't the best idea so I refrained. I ordered a glass of wine, but it went unfinished. And the rest of the week has rolled downhill from there so far.

Even though I'm "doing okay" (meaning I am alive) my life has changed 110% and it sucks and I'm not having a good day... hardly ever. Secrets out. I want the steak. I want to feel normal. I want to eat and enjoy food. And wine. And water. Anyone who knows me, or has seen my ass/chins knows this. I'm a foodie. Or I was. I crave apples now.

Yes, I know what you're thinking... this is a good thing and I should be eating as healthy as possible considering I have Stage 4 cancer and all, but hey, you try getting handed that diagnosis and tell me you're not going to want to do what makes you happy. So what, maybe I'm hangry? But that's just one of millions of other things. For everyone who's asked "how are you" today and gotten an "okay", "not bad" or "hanging in there" response, here's how I really feel, a day in the life. For starters, my head hurts constantly. When I wake up I go pee and it is so dark it's almost brown. But every moment I'm awake I'm drinking water or Gatorade. I'm constantly dehydrated even though I've never drank so many fluids in my life. After the dark and sometimes painful pee, I go to my pill box. It's too full for "regular" medications so I take the over the counter stuff first- ibuprofen, stool softeners, Tylenol. Sometimes I lay back down and cry. Sometimes I just lay back down. From there, usually a good 20-30 minutes to get moving. And by moving, I mean put pants on and brush my teeth. By the time I try to clean up all of the hair from my bathroom sink and pillow that had fallen out along the way, I'm usually ready to sit back down again. (Yes- the hair- it's still coming out. Almost bald. It seems to never end. There is a LOT. I had no idea how much had grown back over the past few months.) Eventually, I'll try to go to the restroom again unsuccessfully. My stomach constantly is in pain. If I'm not nauseous, Its pain. I now have to give myself the "poop shot" which I literally have to give myself with a syringe to make me have a bowel movement every other day. And Every other day it seems worse than the time before. I'm on so many narcotics that my bowels can't function independently. When I take the shot it feels like someone is stabbing me in my gut for at least an hour. I dry heave, or have vomited, at least once every day since last Thursday. I have a ringing in my ears that comes and goes. Usually it just sticks around for a few seconds, nevertheless annoying. My chest constantly feels heavy and when I get up in the morning and have to cough, it feels like my lungs are going to shatter. I have a rash on both of my inner arm creases because I'm only able to sleep on my back and tend to keep my arms folded rather that straight. I guess it creates friction. I try to lay flat with my arms out at my sides but they eventually bend and my hands come together throughout the night. I wake up with my hands crossed, lying on my chest. Just like I would be if I were lying in a coffin.

It's hard not to think about death constantly when you are unsure if you're on the verge of it. If dying isn't something you think about every day, consider yourself blessed. Some days I don't know if I can keep going, but I do. It's days like today when I consider saying "to hell with it" and just living my life naturally, without any medicine or therapies or poisons. But to me that's giving up. Is it? Chemo isn't curing me, I'm "incurable". My miracle will come on its own, right? Why am I putting my body through the torture of all of these medications? It seems like the only option for me, and I struggle with it. Is being strong knowing when to say screw it and see what happens?

While I lay here in bed using every ounce of energy to type this post, some are waiting for an hour in the drive thru at Popeyes because hello, it's

Davenport and nothing that exciting has happened since, well, Sonic probably.. and others are anxiously watching the polls, as if they don't already know who the winning candidate is going to be. I wasn't able to vote today. Just be happy that you have the ability to vote and/or eat Popeyes today…please. I'd give an arm to have done either. I found out from my tests today that my potassium is pretty low. I started taking magnesium a couple weeks ago and the two are supposed to go hand in hand. Doctor decided last week at chemo that I need a break from radiation so I haven't been going for the past couple days. I go back tomorrow, pending more blood test results. I will get a CBC in the AM - hopefully just a finger prick this time. If my platelets are good then I will get radiation. My back pain has gotten better over the past few days surprisingly. Hoping for better days ahead. Thank you for your ongoing prayers! XO

Diane: *What was planned to be a quick one-day drive over to Peoria and back, turned into much more, thanks to the generosity of some wonderful people at the Girl Scouts of Eastern Iowa/Western Illinois (my old place of employment.) My friend Diane, and many others at GSEIWI, collected money from the staff and they chipped in to create a wonderful two-day experience in Peoria, including a Lexus SUV to drive, an overnight stay, dinner, flowers before the performance and wine plus snacks in our deluxe room. Even though Lindsay struggled through the trip, the thoughtfulness of this effort to make a perfect memory with my daughter will always be precious to me and never forgotten.*

Each day was getting a little harder as Lindsay's cancer progressed. Some days I was her sounding board and she would really let loose. I just kept trying my best to stay upbeat for her. Making sure she was taking her meds correctly, had something to eat, kept drinking water. I rubbed and applied lotion to her feet, massaged her hands, gently rubbed her aching body, whatever she wanted. I wanted her mind at ease and her body comfortable. Watching TV together was a distraction we both needed. Taking care of Lola and doing the laundry (mostly PJs) and keeping her house clean, between professional cleanings, kept me busy.

Lindsay's Post 11/19/16

Today is Saturday, November 19th. Yesterday marked 7 months since my diagnosis. Seems like much longer than that. Thanks to all for the positive thoughts and kind notes after my last post. The day after I wrote that post, I decided to stop doing radiation. I also decided that I didn't want to have to give myself injections for the BMs anymore and that I'd rather be in pain than be on a long acting morphine. To me, the bone pain was, and is, "easier" to deal with than the stomach problems. I'm not sure if it was the radiation or the drugs- probably a mix of both- but the overwhelming stomach issues got better right away. I'm able to use the restroom naturally and I have a taste for foods and an appetite again. Sometimes "the remedy is worse than the disease" as they say.

I spent last weekend with friends. I was able to go to the Iowa game and had a great time. I won the soup cook-off with one of my "cancer friendly" chicken tortilla recipes! Who says healthy can't be tasty? The day after I decided to quit radiation last week, my mom and I decided to go on our trip to Vegas that we had to cancel in August because of my emergency surgery. We left Monday and got back yesterday. It's been in my bucket list to see California. So, on Wednesday we went to Long Beach and spent about 24 hours there. I got to see the Pacific. We had a great time in Vegas playing penny slots, enjoying good food, wine, a spa day, riding the Gondola at the Venetian, catching Mat Franco's magic show, and more. We were even spoiled with a surprise limo and champagne at the airport. I continue to be blown away daily by the generosity of so many friends and family members. Most who read this are probably friends with me on Facebook and saw my posts throughout the week so I won't repeat too much but needless to say, we had a great time. Lots of memories made. I felt good for the most part. I did get tired easily and had been dealing with chest pain most of the week.

I had mentioned in my last post how my chest constantly feels heavy and when I get up in the morning and have to cough, it feels like my lungs are going to shatter. It started on the right side but moved over to the left as well. When I woke up this morning it was worse than it's ever been. I could barely take a deep breath and seriously almost screamed in pain when I sneezed. I decided to go get a chest x-ray at Genesis. Of course, we ended up spending almost 4 hours in the ER and I knew I should have waited until Monday to have my oncologist order tests for me. The chest x ray looked fine, but it also looked fine before I found out my cancer has spread to my rib and lung, so I'm not exactly sure what they're looking for in the x ray. All

I know is that it's not normal to feel like someone's sitting on your chest or like you're being stabbed in the sternum when you cough or sneeze. We will see what my doctor has to say about that next week.

I'm still thinking about whether or not to continue with Chemotherapy. I need to talk to my doctor about that next week as well... and understand what the pros and cons are. I know a pro would be not feeling like crap for a week after treatment. And if I've had more progression with this chest pain then while I've been on this treatment, it will be an easy decision for me to say yes I'm going to stop. If the "medicine" aka poison isn't slowing down the progression- what's the point? After we had gone to Northwestern for a second opinion and found out how much the cancer has spread, I think diving into the next therapy was a knee jerk reaction. Lots of thinking and more decisions to be made over the next couple of weeks. I am hoping to feel well enough to get my tree out tomorrow.

I remember that day in September when it was determined that my cancer had metastasized and my oncologist telling us that my expected time to live was 2-3 months. Right away my mind thought "please let it be 3 rather than 2 so I can make it to the holidays". Christmas time is my favorite time of the year. Gosh darn it, it's the most wonderful time of the year! I've been listening to holiday music for a couple weeks. Getting my tree up can't come soon enough. I truly believe I have much more than a few weeks "left", but in the back of my mind that countdown is still there. My anxiety levels are at an all-time high just in general. I can't be in one place for very long and I feel very impatient all the time. I don't believe anyone can put a number on your time here on earth. I still believe in miracles and the power of prayer. This year each holiday we celebrate will be very special to me, starting with thanksgiving next week, and a family weekend getaway a couple weeks after that. May you remember your own blessings as we go into this holiday season as well. XOXO

Diane: *Well, remember when I mentioned a last-minute trip a few posts ago...it happened. She wanted to go to Las Vegas. She wanted to go to the ocean. So, we did it and it was so great. Before we left on Monday, November 14th, there was lots to do to prepare and we made it happen. Lindsay decided what our itinerary would be and she typed it up. Here is what she sent to me:*

Monday
11 AM - Drop Lola at Vet- Bring vaccine info, food, leash
Noon- Airport (Flight departs at 1 PM)
Confirmation #6QR97C Allegiant Air Flight #433, arrive @ LAS 2:25 PM
Check-in @ Cosmopolitan Las Vegas – Booking #YCY6D

Tuesday
Day spent having fun in Vegas!

Wednesday
Check-Out @ Cosmopolitan
9:30 – Airport (11:15 Flight) Southwest Airlines Flight #6596,
arrive @ LGB 12:20 PM
Check-in @ Hyatt Regency Long Beach- Confirmation #30299614

Thursday
Check-Out @ Hyatt Regency Long Beach (check bags at front desk, explore)
2:30 - Airport (4:10 Flight) Southwest Airlines Flight #6111
Arrive @ LAS 5:15 PM
Check-in @ The LINQ Hotel & Casino = Hotels.Com Confirmation #133797169568

Friday
Check-Out @ The LINQ
6 AM – Airport (7:30 Flight)
Confirmation #6QR97C Allegiant Air Flight #432, arrive @ MLI 12:42 PM
Lindsay Pick-up Lola before 3 (scheduled pick-up time 2 PM)

It was a trip of a lifetime! Literally. First, we were surprised by a limo picking us up at the airport (compliments of Krilly, AKA Kristin & Tony Brack) with champagne and everything! We stayed at the Cosmopolitan (a hotel she always wanted to experience) and when we arrived, we were informed that there would be a wait for our room to be ready. When Lindsay walked away from the desk to sit down, I quickly spoke to Ashley, the front desk gal, and explained about Lindsay's situation and how exhausted she was from traveling. I joined Lindsay on the couch to wait and two minutes later the nice lady from the desk came and got us to take us up to our upgraded suite with a balcony overlooking the Bellagio fountains. Not only was it an upgrade, but she had chocolates with a little note delivered to our room, as well. Lindsay posted a picture on Facebook, so I can relate what the note said:

It was a pleasure checking you in, Ms. Thul! Good luck on your road to recovery! Please enjoy this sweet treat on behalf of the Cosmopolitan of Las Vegas and let me know if you need anything.
Sincerely, Ashley, Front Desk

Now that is what I call superior customer service!

Lindsay did her traditional "Hello Las Vegas" overlooking the strip. Those who knew her well, know what I'm talking about. We spent that evening and the next day walking short distances, eating, drinking and gambling along the strip. She was tired and in pain most of the time, but we had so much fun creating these memories. We couldn't go far, but we diligently looked for her favorite slot machines in the casinos. Of course, she did well, as always, at the Blackjack tables. The first morning we were there, Nick had arranged for us to enjoy massages in the spa. So thoughtful! Lindsay really liked lounging under the waterfall and in the warm pool at the spa. It was very calming.

We HAD to try the famous margarita drink at the bar inside the Cosmopolitan. They garnish it with a Sichuan flower, which you are supposed to eat first before sipping the drink. It makes your tongue tingle, then prickle, then numb. Yikes, it was weird, but she insisted, so we did it.

After the first leg in Vegas, we flew to Long Beach, California so that Lindsay could sit on the beach. Soon after we arrived, after checking into the hotel, it was comedic that we knew we were close to the ocean, but we couldn't see it. Someone pointed us in the right direction and we starting walking, and walking, and walking....knowing we would come across the ocean eventually. And we did. Lindsay was so exhausted from walking, she just plopped right down on the sand and stared out across the water, a light breeze blowing the hair on her wig. It was truly magical watching my daughter breath in the salt air, sitting silently, looking up to the Heavens, taking it all in and knowing this was a moment she had dreamed of. I stopped to take several pictures of her there, and I love looking at those now.

121

That night, we had made plans to meet up with my niece, Lindsay's cousin Emily, for dinner. She drove over to Long Beach from LA, where she was staying as part of a TV production, to join us for dinner at (ironically) Nick's on 2nd. Lindsay finally lived the lyrics to a song she loved that night, Cake by the Ocean *by DNCE.*

We wound up our quick trip by heading back to Las Vegas, where we stayed at the LINQ for a night and caught a show. So much fun. Now back to reality and another emergency room visit on Saturday, November 19th.

Lindsay's Post 11/25/16

Today is Friday, November 25th. I hope everyone had an awesome holiday week. Mine has been long! Monday we called my doctor right away to let him know about the increased chest pain and my time spent in the ER Sat. He had me go to Trinity and get a CT scan that morning, then into his office to go over the results that afternoon. The pain that I'm experiencing is in my sternum and moving outwards, which explains why both sides and middle of the chest are hurting. The cancer has spread to my sternum and there are also a few new spots in the lungs. The last scan I had was in October. This progression has occurred in only 6 weeks. I started my new chemo at the end of September. So, this tells me that the chemo is not working. I told my doctor that I did not want to continue with the chemo. He quickly suggested trying another "recipe". I figure it won't hurt to try yet another recipe, I just didn't want to continue with the same one, and assumed we had exhausted all other options. This will be the 6th recipe. I will get that infusion this coming Monday.

Tuesday I was able to get the tree up with moms help! It is not decorated yet- one step at a time. That night I had a great time at friendsgiving... lots of laughs! Wednesday and Thursday were fine. I did not feel well and couldn't go very long without a nap both days. I was able to enjoy time with my niece and family and even got to have a few bites of the thanksgiving meal. Couldn't enjoy it like I would have liked to though. This morning I got to spend some time with my HS bffs Sarber & Velez. We had breakfast at Ross' in Bettendorf. Let's just say it's quite different than It was when it was down by The Travel Lodge or whatever it was called. Sketch. Got to see baby Coop, Skeezy, Shames and the Rollinger's. After breakfast I got to spend time with the Velez's. I feel like I lived at that house in high school and they are a second family to me, so it was really nice getting to hang with everyone. Mayra even led a prayer over me with all the girls and it was really special.

By about 2 PM this afternoon I was exhausted!! Took a nap and woke up with a horrible back pain. The same thing happened this morning. Not sure what's triggering the issue when asleep. Even though I've only done a couple of things each day, I get exhausted super easily and still in a lot of pain. To all friends and family that have wanted to see me this week and didn't: please know that I love you and it's nothing personal. I physically can't schedule things back to back anymore, I just get so exhausted. I'm usually only able to "do something" for a few hours and then I'm ready for bed. I've learned my lesson the hard way that if I push myself and don't listen to my body, it takes days to get back to feeling somewhat normal. There just aren't enough hours in the day anymore it seems like. Sending love, hugs and kisses to all! Have a great weekend.

Diane: *On Tuesday, November 22nd, the Rock Island Rotary Club awarded Lindsay with a Paul Harris Fellow. We had hoped to attend the ceremony, but Lindsay was just not up to it. She had been a North Scott Rotarian for a couple of years but was inactive recently due to her illness. Ruth Lee knew what Rotary meant to Lindsay and she led the effort to bestow this prestigious honor on her.*

On Thanksgiving, Lindsay spent the day at our house playing a few games and resting after more chest pain and testing early in the week, leading to more metastasis being identified.

Lindsay's Post 12/03/16

Today is Saturday, December 3rd. It's been a crazy week since my last post. I had mentioned the back spasms that I was having last Thursday. Those continued to get worse over the next couple of days. Saturday we considered going to the ER but the on call doctor didn't think they would be able to give us anything except the pain meds that I already had at home. Sunday I woke up with literally the worst pain I've ever felt in my life. I was moaning, crying, physically could not contain the pain. And that says a lot because my pain tolerance is pretty high. I rated the pain a 10 out of 10. They immediately gave me some pain meds (again, the same pain meds I'd been taking at home every two hours for the past few days) so that didn't do much. Eventually x-rays and several tests were run. We assumed it was just the cancer.. but I needed pain relief and I needed it right away. I felt like there was an organ that had busted open- something much more than just the cancer pain flaring up. It got to the point where I was not able to breathe. You know, like a baby when they're screaming to get out of the crib but you have to let them cry it out and you feel horrible because they're choking and gagging. They determined that I had pneumonia in my right lung (unexpected and was not coughing or anything, and still unsure if that had anything to do with the pain), and also that my hemoglobin levels were extremely low - about half of what a normal person's should be - and that I needed a blood transfusion.

They also saw a few new spots on my left lung. At this point, it seems like every test or scan that is run just continues to show more spots and lights up like a Christmas tree. So I have to come to terms with the fact that the cancer has taken over my body and I need to be on the strong pain medications 24/7- whether I like it or not. There's no other way to handle the unbearable pain. So they admitted me on Sunday night and the blood transfusion took about 4 hours. I also began several antibiotics for the pneumonia and we kept pumping as many pain meds as possible. My respiration dropped that night because of all the pain meds. It's tricky trying to balance all these drugs and stay on top of the side effects, like not breathing. The next couple of days I was watched like a hawk and had several ups and downs. I was finally released Wednesday afternoon. First thing Thursday I had to go into my oncologist to get the chemo that I had missed on Monday. When I woke up Thursday I was not well at all, but I made it through. This chemo is different because there are 10 pills that I'm taking daily at home, in addition to getting an IV push on the 1st and 8th day of each cycle. Then I have a break (I think 2 weeks), and do that same cycle again. I felt good all day yesterday and so far, so good today. I will never forget this past week. It's the first time I've actually felt like I could potentially die. Between not being able to breathe and the excruciating pain, it's been the worst time I've had thus far in my journey. When you're on the oncology floor and the room next to you has a code blue, then the person on the other side of you is taken to hospice....it makes it all very real. Here's hoping for better days ahead.

Diane: On Sunday, November 27th, Tom met me and Lindsay at the ER. She was in so much pain! Why do they insist on doing all these dumb tests when we know it's just the cancer? Give her the damn pain meds, and not less of a dose than she's already taking for goodness sakes. We went to GMC-Davenport, not realizing Dr. C. wasn't considered on staff there, so he couldn't come and assess her. Next time we would know better.

Lindsay ended up in the hospital for three nights that time as they gave her antibiotics for the pneumonia, gave her a blood transfusion and got her pain under control. I stayed with her the entire time. Tara brought her a cute stuffed puppy because she was missing Lola. Once she was released, she slept her way into December. During her waking hours, she dealt with the pain, took pills, but tried to enjoy her favorite holiday of the year, buying gifts, spending time with family, enjoying her tree and outdoor lights. Saying no to invites, taking care of herself, and getting rest was her top priority right now.

Lindsay's Post 12/12/16

Today is Monday, December 12th. The past week has been pretty good for the most part. Monday we headed to Iowa city to have my 3 month post op check up with the breast surgeon. This was a pretty quick appointment- the surgery areas have healed nicely. We did notice a couple more bumps that have come up along the incision line, similar to those that we noticed when I first started breast radiation. Thursday when we went in to get my day 8 injection, doctor decided to increase my long acting pain medication again. I am getting through longer periods without having to use the breakthrough meds which is nice. Am trying to stay under 20 pills per day and really only take medication if I think I absolutely need it. I usually do ibuprofen and Tylenol when I can. I can feel the back pains and chest pains still but they are becoming more tolerable. The night sweats continue to be something I have to deal with every night which is getting old! I wake up with a wet pillow, but am cold. I have yet to sleep through a full night since I've left the hospital. I took my oral chemo every day last week, and finished the ten day cycle on Saturday. I did start feeling kind of crummy Saturday afternoon and am still not doing the best. I have had a new side effect from the chemo, which I started noticing a couple days ago. Mouth sores. My doctor looks in my mouth and makes sure to check on them every time I see him, but have not had any issues with the past 5 infusions. It's basically just canker sores. So far,

I have one on the side of my tongue, the top left gum area and a little blister on my lip. The mouth sores are more of an annoyance than anything. I've also had a sore throat. It almost feels like it's partly closed, like it's hard to swallow. This has made eating really suck. Even water irritates them. But I'm making sure to continue staying hydrated. Seems like as soon as I get the pain controlled in one area, it pops up somewhere new.

I have had a lot going on, or so it seems like. Even just doing one thing per day is exhausting. I had hung out with friends Wednesday and had family gatherings Friday and Saturday. I am just so exhausted!! Going to spend the rest of today in bed until I have dinner with friends later tonight. Wednesday we have labs and Thursday appointment. Another somewhat busy week unfortunately. It's great seeing family and friends but sometimes I just need a few days alone in my bed. Even though I know I shouldn't feel badly about that, I still do. I'm not used to saying no to people and it seems like it's getting more difficult to do so. But I know my rest is a huge part of my healing process and just hope that my loved ones can understand that and not take it personally. Hoping not to be too drained this week going into the holiday. Love you all XO!!

Diane: *The week before Christmas, a church group came to Lindsay's house to sing carols to her. It had been arranged weeks ahead by a friend of mine. We scheduled it, not knowing how Lindsay would be doing that day. As it turns out she was okay earlier in the day, but later, right before the carolers arrived, she wasn't. She even took a tumble down her stairs, which scared the crap out of me and Kevin. Lindsay falls, the carolers ring the bell, she's crying. Oh dear. I had her stay downstairs and compose herself while I let the carolers in. At least 25 of them!! Finally, she was ready to come upstairs and face Marci and the group of well-meaning carolers. She and I sat on her couch while she held Lola, smiling. Always smiling, even when that was the last thing she wanted to do. She really did enjoy it, though, and it is a blessed memory I will cherish forever.*

Lindsay's Post 12/23/16
Today is Friday, December 23rd. Today my friends came over for a bit. Great time! Yesterday I had my second of this pill/shot blended chemo infusion. No pills to accompany yesterday's injection, although the appointment was followed up with a third radiation simulation! The mouth-

sores are much much better and I am finally able to tolerate eating and drinking most normal things again. That was horrible. One of the worst side effects yet. Thanks for all the ideas you had on helping to manage that pain. Luckily, I know some people in the mouth business and was able to get some mouth rinse that worked! Right when the sores started getting some relief, the reoccurring pain under my left breast becomes more obvious. That pain is now shooting down through my back left leg. I cannot go up the stairs on my left side or put all of my weight on my left leg. Probably doesn't help that I fell down two stairs the other day, but we did some scans just to make sure and it's just the cancer. Mom had stayed with me for a few days this past week after things had gotten pretty bad with all of the different pains. The third round of radiation that we decided on yesterday will (hopefully) help with the pain.

Positive note, my lack of appetite is finally catching up to the steroids and I'm back down 20 lbs. I wouldn't have noticed if I wasn't getting weighed so many times throughout the week. I used to have thoughts that would come to me randomly throughout my crazy busy days. I'd be running from meeting to meeting, sifting junk out of hundreds of emails in-between, and have I'd a "teaching moment" or an "ah-ha!" and jot down a couple notes, usually physically and mentally. I've been doing this for a few years now; compiling "chapters" to my book of life as I go, which I've dreamt of putting into some sort of "how to" piece for successful, young women in business trying to climb that corporate ladder. When I was first diagnosed, I wondered how this new chapter would fit into it. I smiled when I thought about being able to use this as a positive platform for balancing life and work... then (it took me several months to) accept the fact that I wouldn't be working and that fighting this thing is a full-time job. I began having those same "ah-ha" moments as I've been writing on this blog and would jot down a note or two each day to put together when I was ready for a blog update and most of the content would already be there. I've stopped doing that for some reason. I have noticed that I've definitely slowed down, both physically and mentally and the mentally part is what I'm sharing with you today. I will get so tired and it will hit me like a ton of bricks like I need to close my eyes right this second. I'll find myself talking in my sleep or saying things out loud because I'm half-awake, half-dreaming. I will be so knocked out that I wake up unaware of what's going on. This week I forgot what day it was once. Squawked at mom for calling me so early because I thought it was 6 AM but in reality, it was 6 PM. I thought I'd been asleep for 12 hours and it actually had been 2. Brother called half hour later and I still thought it was the next day until I had talked to him for a good couple mins. I was so confused as to why my Christmas lights did not go off on the timer. Then had to call mom back and explain the whole thing and she thought I was crazy. I guess this can be considered a good thing, I definitely need the rest and I sure am getting deep sleeps. I was able to have a few different gatherings with friends and family over the past week and am looking forward to a couple more low key get-togethers as we head into the weekend. Merry Christmas to all! Celebrate the gift of togetherness! Love you!!

Diane: *This was, truly, her MOST favorite holiday of the year. She loved the Christmas lights, putting up the tree, the carols, and all the festivities. The Christmas season meant more to us this year, than ever before. Since Lindsay died, it has been hard for me to put up a Christmas tree in our house each year. But, I do it, trimming the tree with Lindsay's decorations, hanging her stocking, and playing Christmas carols. For her.*

<u>Lindsay's Post 12/28/16</u>

Today is Wednesday, December 28th. I hope everyone had a wonderful Christmas! We are back on the wagon. Began the 3rd round of radiation this week, which is targeting my midback/rib cage area. First breast, then low back, now mid back. The hope is to minimize pain without too many side effects (burns/digestion) as we had with the past two cycles. Tomotherapy, the 360 degree machine that we used the last round on my low back/stomach, is what we are using again this time. Today was day two out of ten. Even though going to the hospital every day isn't fun, I am starting to form a calmness when I'm inside a machine. The tomo radiation machine is more like a CT shape so you're actually inside. It's amazing to me that 8 months ago every day I was in a new machine or doing a new test. In such a short time, my life has almost grown accustomed to being in hospitals and in machines. The machines now comfort me, like a womb almost. Strange and difficult to describe the emotional attachments people get with certain things. I'm supposed to receive 8 more radiation blasts. Prayers for minimal burns and maximum pain relief this time. There's always something. I've stopped wondering what's going to happen next and really am trying to take things day by day.

My friends and family will attest that I cannot make a commitment for something until like an hour before. I truly cannot predict how I will feel ever. I spent Christmas Day on my bathroom floor. The 10 feet away from my toilet that my bed is was almost too far. I was able to spend a couple hours with family on Christmas Eve which was nice, but the rest of the weekend was basically a blur. When I was awake, I was sick. But knew I had to keep drinking and to set alarms to take meds. I continued to have no appetite at all until yesterday-ish. 3 days really with mainly a cheese stick/fruit/cracker only to eat when I took meds. We ordered Olive Garden for Christmas Eve dinner and I wish I could have eaten much more!!!!! So good. Of course, this is mainly just side effects from chemo, which I had on Thursday. It's just frustrating to try to make sense of which drugs do what, what will make me feel certain ways, when and how will I be sick, etc. I am really hoping the mouth sores do not come back!! So that's my fear for today going into the post chemo cycle. The ever-lingering notion of "what if".

My pain has been okay today and today has definitely been the best day I've had since last week as far as comfort. I know that in this grey time though that I need to continue resting and hydrating and not pushing it. Staying away from public crowds to avoid germs, taking medicine (therefore not driving), sleeping when I can, eating, hydrating, etc are things I have to focus on when I'm awake and able to. I have had to miss a lot of important parties and gatherings over the past few weeks which certainly is something I've struggled with... missing memories. I've really been spending a lot of time alone and resting when I can. And I don't want anyone to ever feel sorry for me when I talk about being alone by the way. My mom would live with me right now permanently if I asked her to. Friends and family would be here with me every day and night if I asked them to. I'm so lucky to have that support, but I choose and prefer to be alone sometimes…most of the time. It's a juggling act trying to spend precious time making memories with loved ones, taking care of myself, and staying balanced all at the same time. So, continuing with the one day at a time approach. Highly recommended. I am hoping things continue to go smoothly the next couple of days so I can spend time with friends and family before the holidays conclude officially.

Thank you so so so much to everyone who has sent me holiday cards, gifts, prayers, money, greetings, food, photos, love... every single thought and gesture meant so much to me. Even though my favorite holiday of the year was not a good day for me physically, I think overall the holiday season of 2016 so far has been the best of my life. Life sure is beautiful when you slow down and are present in it. I am feeling blessed and peaceful. Cheers to the next few days of 2016!! XO

Diane: *Christmas came and went......it was so hard knowing it would probably be Lindsay's last one with us, but so joyful at the same time, celebrating little Audrey's very first Christmas. We have a video of her on Christmas Eve being pulled around in the wagon that Kevin and I gave her, with Lindsay's voice in the background. Precious.*

Lindsay went out of her way to buy special gifts for those she loved and she was a trooper through the few family gatherings we had, but you could tell that it was hard on her and she just wanted to be in bed. Some beautiful, professional Thul family photos were taken during the holiday that will be cherished forever.

Lindsay's Post 1/02/17
Today is January 2nd- Welcome 2017! A New year: A feeling of renewal, rejuvenation, positivity, fresh starts. Those that know me know that if you would have asked me last year if there was such thing as having a year worse than 2015 it wasn't possible for me. Then 2016 came and I started realizing that the older I get the less and less right I am all the time. If you would have asked me a few months ago if I would even make it to the new year I wouldn't be able to give you a confident answer. Seems like now the ER visits, hospitalizations, body deterioration issues just keep getting worse. Will one of my hospital visits just end up being the last one someday? Or does everyone go through hospice and have a really firm grip on their timeline as it gets to the end? These are the questions I'm not sure if I want an "answer to" because not every person is the same and also because I was already told I wouldn't live past the holidays and here I am in 2017 going strong. But it's hard. Fucking sucks if you'd really like to know.

This weekend's hospital stay was probably the worst yet- it was better in the sense that I was not in as much pain as I was when I was at a 10/10 a couple weeks ago so it was easier to get under control but it was just humiliating... shitting my pants while puking at the same time without control every 5-10 min. Picture a white bed covered in bright yellow bile. Being bent over literally getting wiped down like a 2 year old who had a blowout. I knew I wouldn't be able to make it in mom's car so this was the first time I traveled by ambulance. They didn't even put me in a coat or hat or shoes before they wheeled me out of my house brrrrr!!! The 8 hour period between when this all started and when I actually got to the hospital were just unimaginable. I couldn't keep anything down. For those who have dry heaved profusely or known what it's like to be barfing without anything coming up know that it is the worst. I kept saying "ok, this can only get better, I don't need to go to the ER. But it only got worse. I can't imagine what it's like for my poor mom to have to watch these things. I couldn't make it to the bathroom, but at least I had a barf bag for the ride over but for about two hours I was just shitting on the hospital bed. Just sitting in it. There was nothing else to do. It was just liquid.

I've for sure mentioned my sweating issues since day one and that's still an ongoing thing. Imagine how that ALREADY dehydrates me constantly. I don't think mom realized how much I was NOT exaggerating when I said my whole bed gets soaked in the night until she witnessed it in my hospital bed at 3 AM when I needed a bed change. I had gotten up to go to the restroom and got out on the wrong side of bed, accidentally ripping my IV out of my hand. Genius. I've never had that type of bleeding. Like it was spraying blood all over so I had to get new bedding anyway. That sucked (IV part) since I'm a hard stick as it is, but man was it nice to get dry bedding half way through the night. I went to bed with stomach pain and bone aches but I was able to have a couple bites of jello and keep that down last night finally and could get to bed around 1-2. They didn't bother me throughout the night as much this time.

Feeling "normal" to me means being able to get out of bed in the morning or doing activities outside the house for more than a day or two in a row. Now that I'm out of the hospital and laying in my own bed without being uncomfortable. I am just so thankful and it is a gift!! Just to be at my house without pain or being over the toilet or needing to be on IVs has got me feeling happy currently. For those having "back to work" anxiety tonight - let it go! Be grateful that you have a job and are healthy and comfortable. Something so small that I was so used to doing everyday like getting through a movie or bathing are privileges. I think back to what my life was like pre-diagnosis and I see people living these normal lives and I just get really frustrated that I can't force anyone to know how it feels. I wouldn't wish this experience upon my worst enemy but I do wish just for a day or two that people could take a peek into "a day in the life" or one of these nightmare hospital visits where you aren't sure if you'll make it. The world would be such a better place if we all could all be truly thankful just for being alive and well and remove yourself from anything that doesn't matter.

Tomorrow I have to reconnect with radiation doctor and oncologist office to see what additional appointments or changes are in my schedule this week after this past episode but I'm really hoping to zoom through radiation to get this over with (should be 7 treatments left). Not sure how I'm feeling about this chemo- it has been a rough few weeks since I've started this 6th recipe. BUT I am trying to stay positive and know that these unbearable side effects mean that something is working inside there. Good, bad, or indifferent- I think I'd rather feel like crap in hopes of knowing that the poison I'm getting is attacking some cancer cells in there. I'll puke and sweat all day long if it means I'm getting rid of cancer cells from my body.

I have been continuing to deal with new pains of course, and know that there's probably cancer wherever the pain occurs. I think I mentioned my left arm giving me problems and that pain has moved up to my shoulder area and down below my butt. There's always something! This thing is just taking a tour around my body. Please continue praying!!!

I am so grateful for my parents!! Even though dad hates puke, he stayed in there with me anyway and held my hand. Every time I'm sick all I want to do is hold my dad's hand and he's always there to let me. I asked him why this is happening to me last night and he said it's just part of my plan.

My poor mom has a cold of her own but didn't leave my side all night. At least Trinity has "pull out" beds unlike Genesis and U of I where she had to sleep in a chair for 3 nights. I can't help but to be happy for the time I'm getting with my loved ones, even if it's in a hospital.

Now on to tackle this new year. Those insurance companies do not mess around. I already had the first co-pay of 2017 today for a prescription. I had hit my deductible and out of pocket stuff last summer and still was working full time at that point. Now that it's a fresh start, even though I'm still able to pay for cobra monthly, that on top of starting over with all the expenses for the year gives me so much anxiety. A friend of mine showed me this website where cancer patients can write/blog and get paid! Not sure the details- I need to look into that and some other side gigs to get through. I sold one of my LV purses the other day for $1k so that's something else I'm going to keep doing is purging my closet room. It will be all good. Thanks to all of you, I know I will be okay and am trying hard to meditate and keep calm every day. Can't wait for my trivia benefit coming up the Sunday after next. I wish for nothing but happiness, health, love, kindness and prosperity for each of you in the new year! XO

Diane: *January started out bad and got worse as Lindsay continued to deteriorate quickly. Lindsay was always feeling sick those days and had another unplanned hospital visit over New Year's. She was so ill that we had to call an ambulance. It took me awhile to convince her to go and I know it's because she was afraid that she won't make it back home again. The hospital visits were becoming second nature now. The same questions, the difficulty drawing blood, me trying to sleep on a chair or pull out, helping Lindsay in and out of bed to the bathroom with her IV pole. At least I could be there for her. That was my blessing.*

Those weeks are a blur in my memory and I may be a bit off on what comes next. My sister, Donna, and niece, Emily, came by one day to see Lindsay and put away her tree and Christmas decorations, which was a huge help to us! Two more hospital stays were coming this month and at this point, Lindsay wasn't able to type her posts on her phone anymore, so she asked me to do it.

Diane Posted for Lindsay 1/07/17

Today is Saturday, January 7th. This is Diane, writing for my daughter, Lindsay. Due to several new issues she is experiencing, it is hard for her to make a journal post today. Acknowledging I am not the writer she is, I will do my best to keep you informed if Lindsay can't. You may see me writing on here per Lindsay's request every now and then, especially after what has occurred the past few days. Since returning home from the hospital this past Monday, she had been doing pretty well for a couple days there. She was extremely tired after getting out of the hospital Monday and slept for the next day. She went to radiation on Wednesday and Thursday, but mostly slept those days too, her pain slightly bearable. She did notice increasing body pains later in the week. On Friday morning, we went to see oncologist, not knowing what he would want to do next. Well, after a complete exam, evaluation of the new pain she is experiencing in her pelvis; lower extremities; and arms, it was determined that this most recent chemo recipe wasn't working to slow down or stop the cancer's unrelenting progress. Not great news, but something we had already realized. Her pain level is no longer controlled by what she is currently prescribed. Dr. leaned over and very caringly told Lindsay today that he didn't feel there was anything further that could be done and he didn't want her to have to deal with treatment side effects when treatments continued to fail. He really cares so much about her, as does his entire staff.

Along with the pain in her pelvis and lower extremities, Lindsay is experiencing weakness in her legs and there have been a couple times when her legs gave out from under her. Dr. asked again about her living situation and stated that it was time to have someone with her 24/7 (me), and that he thought it best to involve Hospice at this point. He explained that a Hospice nurse would come into the home as needed, evaluate her and report directly to the Dr. on her status. The nurse would also be able to do some pain control and other treatments at home to keep her comfortable, like IV fluids when needed. Additionally, to get her pain better under control, he decided to once again increase her pain meds, doubling the long acting one and the short acting, every two hours as needed.

Well, after leaving the oncology office Friday morning, amidst tears by the staff, Lindsay and myself, we headed home to have a bite to eat and rest and take in this new information. A couple hours later after picking Lola up from the groomer, I left Lindsay in good spirits and alert as I went into work. She was tired and ready for a rest. I ran home to change and planned to be at work for a couple hours until my husband could relieve me. A few hours later, I was kicking myself for leaving her and knew that something wasn't right. When I returned a little after 7:00 PM, I found my girl basically unresponsive - but breathing - laying half on and half off her bed. At max I could only get her to open her eyes and "respond" for seconds at a time. When she did talk to me, her words made no sense. She was confused and lethargic, her eyes kept rolling up. It was very scary. Not knowing what to do and not feeling as though another 911 call was warranted, I contacted Lindsay's step-sister who is a medical professional. She immediately came to her house and did an evaluation. After speaking with the oncologist on call, we got her into the car and drove her to UnityPoint, Bettendorf for the 2nd time in less than a week. Thank you, Abbey for your help and expertise!! We were admitted last night, and luckily were able to come home this afternoon. She is still very out of it at times and says things that don't make sense/talks in her sleep- but she knows what's going on. She is sitting next to me in her chair right now and her pain is controlled at the moment. Better yet, she is AWARE and not confused. I am all set up in the bedroom (moved the downstairs guest bed/frame upstairs into what used to be her "craft room") next to hers to move in.

The family will meet the Hospice nurse on Monday and are hoping for more information on how it works. We are doing good right now just resting and asking for your prayers. Hope you are having a good weekend.

Diane: *Getting Hospice lined up and on a schedule, coordinating delivery of hospital equipment, trying to keep Lindsay comfortable and making yet another hospital visit kept me busy and I felt sometimes like I was losing my mind. Honestly, I was mad. Mad at my family for not helping me (at least that's what I was thinking to myself), mad at God, just MAD. My daughter was dying right before my eyes and I was also very scared.*

135

We talked about whatever Lindsay wanted to talk about. What she wanted to happen after she passed. Who she felt up to seeing or talking to. She enjoyed the couple times that my sister, Debbie, came and sat with her. At the hospital and at her house. My sister is a mental health professional and I think Lindsay felt like she could talk about the really hard things with her. Like, what's it like to die? Will I know when it will happen? I'll be forever grateful to my sister for being there for Lindsay during that time. Other times we just watched TV together and she dozed off and on. Sometimes, when she was sleeping, she'd make weird sounds. That scared me, too.

Lindsay's feet were a mess and she wanted a pedicure so bad. We scheduled one, but ended up canceling, like many other things, because she just wasn't up for it. She just wants to hang in there, and feel good for her next fundraiser, Slay Squad Trivia, and little AJ's first birthday. She was determined.

Diane Posted for Lindsay 1/19/17

Today is Thursday, January 19th. This is Lindsay's Mom, Diane again. Lindsay is now having some vision problems in addition to the fuzzy-headedness that caused me to be the guest writer last time. I'm sure you've noticed it's been nearly 2 weeks since the last post. We've had a lot going on! I mentioned in the last post how the 6th chemo recipe wasn't working. We're officially out of treatment options unless by some miracle we can get into/find a clinical trial, which all the Doctors are continuing to work on... we all do.

Hospice services began last week with initial consultation/admission on Monday, January 9th. All is going well with them so far. It really is a load off my mind to know we can just pick up the phone, day or night, if we need something. They delivered several medical equipment items Lindsay will need now or in the near future: wheelchair, walker, shower chair and oxygen. Everything is being taken care of by Hospice – including medications - as needs occur, which is really great. This program is a godsend. It was time.

Lindsay continues to have periods of confusion and disorientation at times and she seems glad to have me here full-time. I've noticed that she has more difficulty keeping her thoughts straight and sometimes is slow to comprehend and form sentences at times. But with me here, she seems more relaxed and less worried about falling, taking medications correctly, etc... She has had a couple of small falls and times when she cannot get up or climb steps on her own. Her ever-so-sacred independence is quickly disappearing each day and I can see how much that bothers her. Understandable. I try very hard not to "hover", but it's hard.

The Hospice nurse is coming 2 times a week right now. That can change at any time. Lindsay's dad is coming over to spend time with Lindsay on Friday afternoons now which she really looks forward to. A couple of very close friends are also taking turns coming and sitting with her to give me a break a few times a week. She is very tired and it is hard for her to stay alert for long periods, so we keep it short. She continues to make plans with family and friends, even though she winds up cancelling quite often due to tiredness, nausea, pain...any number of things that keep her down. And she HATES that. She just wants to spend time with people she loves, but unfortunately, it's not always possible.

Last Saturday she was so happy to spend time with her friends Sarah & Amanda (and baby Cooper), even though she ended up vomiting near the end of the visit. She says "sorry ladies!" Ha! No, they didn't mind. On Sunday, it was a big day for Lindsay. A third benefit (SlaySquad Trivia) was held to raise money for Lindsay's ongoing expenses. She was able to attend for a couple of hours and was so happy to be there and see everyone. So much love and support was shown for this girl of ours. THANK YOU to everyone, especially Jacqueline who initiated and spearheaded the event! We beat our goal by almost $10k! My amazing daughter-in-law, Tara set up an online Meal Train so that people could sign up to bring me and Lindsay meals each day. The schedule filled up immediately for the next 6 weeks! Again, we are overwhelmed by the love! It's really been a blessing!

Today we had a visit with the oncologist. Lindsay has been in A LOT of pain this past week. Even the massive doses of pain meds aren't keeping the pain under control. Time for a change. Again. He increased the long acting medicine and then ordered a PCA (Patient Controlled Analgesia) pump. She will have a button to push to provide immediate pain meds as needed. We are happy about this and fingers crossed it helps the pain get under control!

We are looking forward to this weekend and hope she will be able to participate in a couple of family events, including little Audrey's first birthday party. We love you all and cannot express adequately how much we appreciate everything you are doing for Lindsay and our family, be it a meal, call, text, visit, prayers or positive thoughts. THANK YOU!

Diane: *January 15th - Trivia went great! So many people were there in support of Lindsay. And Lindsay, intent on NOT using the wheelchair and talking to everyone, made sure everything was running right and helped set up the silent auction. She was so tired and sick, but she hung in there for about half the event. The highlight for Lindsay (and me) was the video created by Lindsay's friend Rachel with everyone sending in video greetings, I Love Yous and get well wishes. What a loving effort!*

On Sunday, January 22nd, only 10 days before she died, Lindsay was able to attend Audrey's first birthday party at Nick and Tara's house. My parents and my sister Donna were there, along with many other family and friends, and they loved being able to see and talk to Lindsay. So many cherished memories being made and photos we will cherish forever.

On Tuesday, January 24th, Lindsay wanted my BFF Debbie to come over for a movie and play a game. We had fun just hanging out, but it took a toll on Lindsay and she wasn't able to hang out for long before going to bed.

On the night of what would be her final trip to the hospital, she was having hallucinations. Aside from the night she died, this was the worst time for me. I was at a breaking point, trying to handle her during this day/night where she was hearing and seeing people, convinced they were hiding in her house and demanding to go outside so she could yell for them. Then later, I had to physically try to restrain her as she was wanting to leave the house, or use her phone to call who-knows-who? She was so out of it and they said it was the morphine. At one point she got her phone away from me and called 911, telling the dispatcher that her mom was hurting her. They had to follow-up and came to the house while I was trying to contact Tom and the Hospice nurse to come ASAP. The Davenport police showed up (two of them) and went into Lindsay's bedroom to talk to her. They could tell right away that she was hallucinating and in the living room, I was bawling and trying to explain to the officers that she was late-stage breast cancer and on enough morphine to bring down two horses.

They were very understanding and the one officer told me he had dealt with his mom dying from cancer. They were so understanding and nice. As soon as they left, she was still combative with me, but Tom showed up soon after and he laid in bed with her, keeping her calm. Then the Hospice nurse arrived, thank GOD! She talked to Dr. C after making an assessment and we took another trip to the hospital in an ambulance where they kept her a couple of days to alter her pain meds.

Lindsay's dad, Tom, had made arrangements for the St. John Vianney priest, Father Verba, to give Lindsay the Anointing of the Sick, but as it turns out, she was in the hospital at the time they had arranged, so Father came to Trinity Bettendorf to see her. Anointing of the Sick, AKA Last Rites. Tom and I were with her and Father V. placed his blessings on us, as well. I think it really made Lindsay peaceful, being anointed with Holy oil, knowing she was absolved of all her sins and that her soul would be welcomed into Heaven.

Finally, she was set to be discharged from the hospital, and we arranged for a hospital bed to be delivered to her house. It would be necessary for her safety as she continued to decline. She wasn't happy about this, but the guys tore down her bed and in came the hospital bed. The side rails made me more at ease, but with her being hooked up to the oxygen and the pain meds pump, it was a chore to maneuver her out of bed and into the bathroom, so the commode was now being used. She didn't eat much after she got home (maybe a popsicle or piece of apple) and slept most of the time. She was visited by both Nick and Tara in the days leading up to her death. Some special one-on-one time that I know they all cherished.

These last few days of Lindsay's life are a bit unclear in my memory. It's like I was living in this vacuum, trying to keep Lindsay comfortable, trying to get through the days. I had her medication schedule on my phone set with a reminder because there were so many pills and so much to remember. She hated the oxygen tube, forgot to push her pain meds button, wasn't eating much - if anything at all, and overall sank into mostly sleep, counting on me for everything she needed. She deteriorated so quickly, but stayed lucent for the most part. Thank goodness for Hospice. I called them almost daily and they became very familiar with us. They were so great with Lindsay.

On Tuesday, January 31st, Tom spent some time with Lindsay as I took a short break to have lunch with my friend, Debbie. I mostly remember that she was in and out of it for the most part during the day, and I had to keep hitting her pain pump for her, but it was barely helping. Luckily, her commode was close to the hospital bed and the oxygen was helping with her breathing.

The hospice nurse came and went several times that day. They were so amazing! In the afternoon, I received a call from Dr. C's office. He wanted to swing by Lindsay's house to see her after finishing with his office patients. As it was, the hospice nurse happened to be there when he arrived, accompanied by our dear friend (and his nurse practitioner) Megan Pikuza. Lindsay was so happy that he made that effort! She was smiling and joking with him as he sat on the edge of her hospital bed and assessed her in her bedroom, with Lola licking him on her bed. After conferring with the hospice nurse, another increase in her pain medicine was ordered. They said "see ya" to each other and Dr. C. stopped to speak with me in the living room. I needed to ask the hard question, but didn't know how to phrase it. He understood and said that he was amazed at how cognitive and alert she was on such high doses of pain meds. He was shocked that she was able to carry on the conversation she had just had with him. He seemed incredibly sad and dejected, as he softly told me that it would only be a couple days, a week at most. NO!!!!! I'm not ready. But I knew she was.

I made the call to Tom and Nick to let them know what Dr. C had told me. They weren't able to accept this either. Tara had just left (unwillingly) on a business trip and this was her fear. I was so happy that she had been able to spend some quality time with Lindsay earlier that week before her trip. I tried to assure Nick that it wouldn't be that quick and she'd hang in until Tara got back, but he was kicking himself that he had encouraged her to go. I shared with my ex-husband that my biggest fear at this point was that she would die in the middle of the night, when no one else was there, and I wouldn't be able to handle it, not know what to do. I was so scared. I was kind of hoping that I would have some way of knowing it was going to happen, and I could call for help.

After he closed the Grape Life, Kevin stopped by to see us that evening around 8:30. Of course Lindsay hadn't eaten anything - she hadn't really for days. I had some food from someone who dropped off for the meal train that night and shared it with Kevin. Lindsay's TV was on, which it was most of the time when she was in and out of sleep. She liked it on.

Before he left, Kevin chatted a bit with Lindsay, gave her a hug and told her he loved her. She said the same thing back and as he was exiting her bedroom, Lindsay said "would you close the door, please." Kevin needed to get home and take care of our dog, Sadie, but we sat and talked in my room for a few minutes, listening to Lindsay groaning with each breath. It was so loud. He hugged and kissed me and left to go home.

Throughout the night, Lindsay would sit straight up in bed and pull at her oxygen tube in her nose. She hated it. I had to make her put it back in. She tried to get up from her hospital bed with tubes attached to use the commode several times. She nearly pulled out her IV. I was afraid to leave her alone that night as she was so agitated and moaning and getting up without notice, even though she was really out of it. I didn't want her to fall or pull out tubes or anything. So finally, after getting up multiple times during the night, I just resigned myself to the chair we had moved next to her bed (where I sat and we watched TV together) so that I could keep an eye on her and help her if needed. I eventually fell asleep in that chair and was awakened for the last time by Lindsay sitting up straight in bed, throwing her legs over the side and pulling out her nasal cannula. It was February 1, 2017 at approximately 2:00 AM.

As she started to stand up, I grabbed her and backed her onto the commode, which was by her bed, up next to her dresser. Sitting for a moment, she was looking off and not responding to me. She stretched out her arms and legs, as if she was reaching, and took a couple of very ragged breaths. Her breathing slowed as she took her final breaths. First one, then I realized what was happening. NO, NO, NO, NO, I sobbed. I love you, Mommy's here, as I held her up in a sitting position. I love you baby girl, it's okay, I'm here, it's okay.

Did she understand what was happening? Was she scared? I didn't think so. Her face was peaceful. I was terrified.

One more breath and whoosh it all left her body, her eyes closed, she went limp in my arms. My daughter was dead, in my arms, her head fallen back against her dresser. I had her body in my arms, trying desperately not to let her body fall to the floor, sobbing. No, no, no. I love you. I had to get to my phone, but where was it? It was in the chair next to her bed. I made sure she wouldn't fall and quickly grabbed my phone. I can't remember who I called first, Kevin or Tom? They both needed to get there ASAP.

I realized the front door was locked and there would be no way for them to get in. I couldn't leave her, she could fall to the floor, but I had her against the dresser and took the chance to run down to the front door and unlock it. My head couldn't register that she had passed away, but my sub-conscious brain set me into action. I knew there were things I needed to do, I could fall apart later. I couldn't move her alone and I wanted her back in her bed. I think Kevin got there first, but we couldn't move her, the weight was too great. I just wanted her off that commode. She deserved a little dignity at this time. I felt she was hovering above us, watching what we were doing with her body. I still felt her in the room. I couldn't stop sobbing and holding her. Tom and Mary got there and we all tried, but realized we weren't going to be able to move her back into her bed, so we did the best we could by lowering her to the floor, straightening out her limbs, covering her body.

Lola was suddenly in the room and climbing on her, licking her face. I knew that Lola needed to do that, to kiss her, say good-bye. And I know that Lindsay would love having Lola on her, licking her face and head, just like she always did while she was sick. I called Nancy, Tara's mother, before I called Nick. I had to be sure that she could go over to their house and stay with Audrey before I could ask Nick to come. It was 2:30 in the morning. That call to Nick was the hardest, I think. When he arrived, he could only look at her from the doorway of her bedroom. I couldn't stop hugging her and kissing her.

I noticed as she was laying there, that she had bit her bottom lip during death. She was still warm and she looked like she was sleeping, but I had to carefully remove her lip from between her teeth. I asked Mary to go into her closet and find some clothes for her to send with the funeral home guys. She wanted a closed casket, so nothing fancy, no make-up, no wig. By then I had contacted the hospice nurse on call and she arrived quickly, then took over, calling the funeral home and Dr. C. She was amazing and took control. All I had to do was caress and kiss my daughter. I kept telling myself this was just her body. She had gone to be with the Angels in Heaven now.

PART 3 - AFTER

<u>FINAL GoFundMe POST by Nick 2-2-17</u>

Today is Thursday, February 2nd. This is Lindsay's brother, Nick. Unfortunately, as most people know, Lindsay passed away early yesterday morning after a very hard fought battle with inflammatory breast cancer. To say she was an inspiration of strength and perseverance would be an understatement. Thank you to everyone that has taken the time to make a donation, whether it be monetary or physically through kind words, food, calls, everything, you all will never know the amount of support she felt and we felt. It is an extremely difficult time for our family, but knowing Lindsay is now in peace and comfort makes it a little better. We can never, ever express our gratitude through this time, but know that every one of you made a difference and helped Lindsay smile through the pain. Thank you all, from the bottom of our hearts.

Diane: *Preparing for your daughter's funeral is something no parent should have to do, but I knew what she wanted. She had died as she wanted, in her home with at least one loved one with her. Of course, we chose the pink casket with the beautiful satin lining. Some of her favorite men served as pall bearers. In a matter of hours, we were writing the obituary, with help from the funeral home, and planning the service, with help from the priest that had given her the Anointing just a few weeks before. The funeral home kept her casket opened for us to take one more look at our beloved Lindsay prior to the visitation starting the afternoon of February 3rd, but I think Kevin and I were the only ones that came close. I reached out to touch her one more time and Kevin stopped me. I get it. It was just her body.*

She really didn't want us to have a visitation and she definitely wanted a closed casket. She told me this after we attended the funeral of one of her grade-school friends a few months earlier. She didn't want everyone standing in line, crying, being sad. The family overruled her on this one. We knew that so many people who loved Lindsay, who loved and knew our family, would want to come and give us their condolences. This was more about those left behind to grieve, giving them an outlet to mourn and share stories.

So, we did the one thing she asked us not to do and some people waited in line for 3 hours. Hundreds and hundreds of wonderful people showed up to pay their respects, give us a hug, and talk about the wonderful person that was our daughter, our sister, our aunt, our cousin, our granddaughter, our niece, our friend.

The funeral was held the following day, on Saturday, February 4th at St. John Vianney Catholic Church, where Lindsay had been baptized, received First Holy Communion and was confirmed. As Tom and I walked in with her casket, followed by Kevin and Mary, Nick and Tara, I sensed the hundreds of people who had come from near and far (including my brother from Idaho and our friends from Florida) for this sad day when we would lay Lindsay to rest. The church was packed full with people who loved her, from her pre-school teacher, to old neighbors and co-workers and the Hospice nurses, to Dr. C and his wife. I heard this later, but was told he never attended the funerals of patients he'd lost. That made it even more meaningful to us - that he had come to love her, too. The services are a blur; I just remember staring at her coffin sitting in the center of the church, draped in the white pall, thinking about her body inside. I also remember looking up at the skylight above the alter and seeing what looked to be a Dove flying around with the sky and clouds in the background. I imagined that it was Lindsay's spirit.

Driving to the cemetery in the limo was surreal. The spot we had chosen was covered with a bright blue canopy, and blue covered chairs were set up in front for the family. The guys gently moved Lindsay from the back of the hearse and carried her to the mechanism ready to lower her into the ground. It's interesting how they drape this part so that it is hidden, but you know what is under the drape - the mechanism to lower the coffin into a big hole in the ground. It was February and it was cold, but I didn't feel it. Then the snow began gently to fall and it felt like the entire experience was being orchestrated by Lindsay. You could just feel her presence – in the church and here at the cemetery. I think the

144

priest said some prayers, gave Tom and me a blessed crucifix - like the one we placed in her coffin - and then everyone shuffled up to say their goodbyes. Everyone was weeping at this point, knowing that this was it. Tom broke down at the coffin. It was probably not the first time, but it was the only time I saw it. He had been so strong and my heart was in pieces as I consoled him. She was Daddy's girl. Everyone took a flower from the beautiful bouquets brought from the church, and I hugged the people who loved her most after they said good-bye to Lindsay.

As friends and family members gathered at the Grape Life following the services and luncheon at the church, the most amazing and memorable thing happened. Little Audrey, who was just a week or so past her first birthday, walked hand-in-hand with her aunt Rachel over to the large, framed picture of Lindsay we displayed at the visitation and funeral, leaned in and gave her aunt Lindsay's picture several kisses. Someone caught it on video. It is one of the most precious, heart-warming acts of love I have ever witnessed.

Since Lindsay's death so many things have occurred. Choosing her burial plot and picking out her headstone was a joint effort, but we went with pink marble, engraved with her name and butterflies. I decided to buy the plot next to hers, so that one day, we can lay side-by-side like we did so many times through the years, and sadly during her illness. Of course, I'll be on her right, as she instructed every time we took pictures together.

Lindsay's beloved dog, Lola, came to live with me, Kevin and our dog, Sadie. The two of them love being together every day, and Sadie truly enjoys laying around or playing with her sister/companion. I cannot even imagine how they ever got along without each other!

We decided to hold an online auction to divest of her possessions that didn't get claimed by one of us. I wanted those closest to her to have some of her things, especially if they had some meaning, like a picture or a piece of clothing, a purse or some jewelry. My brother-in-law Brent, owner of Wears Auctioneering, and niece Emily did such a good job with the online auction. The toughest part for me was cleaning out her closet room. I think there were five of us who worked on it for multiple days. The first day we started this process, all the family was there to help. Tom was in charge of taking all of her purses and cleaning them out – which took a while since they ALL still had stuff in them. We were getting ready to turn the house back over to the bank and so everything needed to be removed.

145

One of our customers who lived near Lindsay's house, Greg Sacrison, made sure Lindsay's yard stayed tidy once spring arrived. It would take months to get the auction completed, the house cleaned and turned back over to the bank.

Much of her professional clothing was donated to Dress for Success and some of us took boots or purses or items of clothing we liked and would use. About a week after the funeral, I decided, against my better judgment it turns out, to go over and do some more purging, sorting and cleaning at Lindsay's house. Mistake. It was eerie being there alone. No Lindsay's bigger-than-life personality, no TV, no music, no Lola barking. Just quiet. I had spent so much time in that house with her! I sat on the floor in her bedroom for a bit. The medical equipment company had come and picked up the bed, etc…so the bedroom was empty except for her dresser (yes, the dresser I propped her on after she died – more memories). While I could still feel her presence in that house, I moved to the closet room and started packing up more stuff to donate and came across a fanny pack. I was sure that Tom had gone through all of the purses and such, but for some reason, I unzipped the side pocket and found two little gold charms with pictures of four or five-year-old Lindsay in them. You know, the ones we got in a photo package when we took the kids for annual pics at JC Penney. People my age will remember these. I don't know how or why she had these in a fanny pack that I thought had been gone through, but I lost it. It felt like she was reaching out to me. I literally broke down sobbing and knew I needed help ASAP. My husband, Kevin, was out of town for work. Nick was out of town and Tara was taking care of Audrey. My bestie, Debbie, was unavailable (can't remember why), my sister Debbie was at work. So, I called Tom's cell. Mary answered and they were in the car going somewhere, but quickly changed direction and headed to Lindsay's house to bail me out. I was a mess, but they were calm and hugged me and stayed to help do some more packing of Lindsay's possessions.

Birthdays, family and friends' weddings, new babies, life goes on and although it has gotten a little easier for me, I still miss her SO MUCH and know I always will. The first year or so after her death, I was thinking about her every minute of every day, or so it seemed. Missing her to the depths of my soul, feeling this huge hole in my heart. It took a long time to get that night out of my mind and out of my dreams. I remember one day it occurred to me that I was thinking of her dying less and less, and thinking about her LIFE more and more. I realized this was a turning point. I began to rely less on Xanax to sleep and keep me from *crying all the time, and turned my energies into helping create an annual golf outing to raise money for IBC research and education.*

Working at the Grape Life every day was tough, since Lindsay had spent so much time there with us. But also, I never knew who was going to walk through the door and want to talk about Lindsay. Even people I didn't know, who had followed her story or knew her from something or somewhere, or didn't know her at all but had heard her story. It was so hard to try and smile and be upbeat all the time when all I wanted to do was bury myself under my covers and cry. But then I thought about HER and what she endured and I realized I had to suck it up and if I cried in front of customers, or was a CHIB (Lindsay's word) because I was mad at the world, then so be it. There were several times when people I didn't know saw Lindsay's picture at the GL and said they knew her or followed her posts, or simply knew someone that knew her. It was crazy the reach her story had. I just hope and pray it was for good and that if even ONE LIFE is saved because of what Lindsay went through, then it will be for good.

We continue to have a #slaysquad team each year for Komen's event and Nick kept her Facebook account alive as a remembrance page. I encourage you to check it out. My heart just melts and I am filled with pure joy whenever someone posts a memory or a picture. I've also been visiting her grave less and less. At first, it was daily, because it was where I felt closest to her. But then, weekly, now once or twice a month. Again, seeing activity at her grave makes me so happy.

A few months ago, during the slow times of the summer of 2019, it dawned on me one day that I could be doing more with my life than sitting around waiting for customers to buy wine or slapping a fake smile on my face to chit chat with people who walked through the doors of our business. I could literally hear Lindsay telling me to DO SOMETHING MORE. So, one day, I was searching jobs online, using the words cancer and hospice. With my medical background, my 20 years in non-profit leadership and adding in my personal experiences with cancer, I knew there was something out there where I could MAKE A DIFFERENCE. I knew this because Lindsay was telling me it was so, and I began to believe it myself. On a whim, I completed an online application for a position at Genesis Health System's Cancer Care Institute, dusted off my resume, which hadn't been in circulation for over six years, uploaded it and waited. HR called me the next day. I now have this great 32-hour per week job enrolling women in an early cancer detection program and managing a free mammography program for uninsured and underinsured women. Bonus - I get to talk about Lindsay every day.

I've always said, I just don't want her to be forgotten. This is my biggest fear and another reason I decided to make this book happen.

A group of women who knew and loved Lindsay brought others together at the Grape Life on March 7th, to reminisce and share stories of Lindsay. It was amazing. I'll never forget how my sister, Debbie, got up in front of 40-50 people (something that is completely out of character for her) to recall the last time she spoke to Lindsay. She was past the point of seeing friends and having casual visitors, and she told of how Lindsay felt so guilty and sorry that she had to turn people away. Debbie wanted these people to hear that Lindsay loved them all so much and was so sorry she might not have given them the chance to see her one more time and say good-bye.

A second Slay Day was held a year after the first one, on June 25, 2017, back at Public House. This time we celebrated the life of a beautiful soul and held a pink balloon release into the sky. I swear I saw her face in the clouds smiling down on us and took a picture to capture the vision. Lindsay's SLAY cap, and a photo of her and Nick taken at the first Slay Day, remain on display at one of her favorite places, Public House.

As I mentioned earlier, we started the Lindsay Thul Memorial Golf Outing, which is held annually around her birthday at Glynns Creek Golf Course where Lindsay's friend Deanna's husband, John, is the golf pro. Proceeds have been donated to the IBC Network Foundation, where Lindsay first turned when she was diagnosed. They are doing great things, supporting research projects focused on Inflammatory Breast Cancer. Maybe someday we will have some answers.

I show Audrey pictures of Lindsay every time I'm with her and she ALWAYS knows who she is, whether it was Lindsay as a young girl or going through cancer treatment. Audrey knows it's her Aunt Lindsay. Last Easter, it was a beautiful day and my sister Donna and family brought my aging parents to our house. Someone suggested that we drive over to the cemetery and visit Lindsay. My parents had not gone to the cemetery after the funeral, so this would be their first time. Audrey, then 3 years old, said she wanted to go see Lindsay, too! It was heart wrenching and so sad when she questioned where she was when we got to the cemetery. We explained that we were at Lindsay's Place, *and she seemed to accept that.*

Right before Christmas this year, on December 19, 2019, I received a message from a friend of Lindsay's named Amanda. I had held her bridal shower at the Grape Life after Lindsay died. She now lived in Denver and had recently had a beautiful baby boy. We are friends and keep up with each other on Facebook, and when she reached out, it was to ask me for help. Her husband's cousin, Vanessa age 32, was recently diagnosed with Inflammatory Breast Cancer. My heart sank, but then I thought – I can help this family! Amanda connected me with Vanessa's mother and we talked on the phone. She immediately asked how my daughter was doing and I had to tell her something that I knew would be extremely difficult for this Mom to hear, that my daughter had died ten months after her diagnosis. Not something I wanted to have to tell her, but I knew she had to hear it and NOT DELAY in getting Vanessa to an IBC specialist – preferably in Houston at MD Anderson. I was so happy and relieved to hear from Vanessa's Mom after Christmas that they were getting her down to Houston. This was truly the first time I felt like Lindsay's journey could really save someone else's life. This is truly her legacy.

We see cardinals every day and many find dimes or pennies in the most unique places, associating that with Lindsay. I love to read memories and see pictures of her pop up on social media and especially appreciate all those that reach out to me in texts or messages on those difficult days, like her birthday (October 5), Christmas (her favorite holiday), Mother's Day, the day she was diagnosed (April 18), and the day she died (February 1).

We have all learned so much from Lindsay's journey. I think her friend Jackie summed it up best when she wrote the following on November 28, 2019:

Your diagnosis has shown me what the true definition of bravery is. Every single day, you wake up, and you choose to fight. You fight hard. You fight until you are completely exhausted. You have shown me the meaning of strength, not only in the physical form, but also mentally, and spirituality. You have shown me how to be persistent and persevere. You have shown the world how to be selfless and caring; throughout your journey you have made it a mission to educate women on IBC - to share every single step of your path - hoping that it saves another woman from having to follow in your footsteps.

I saw Jackie recently, when she was visiting Davenport and she stopped by the Grape Life. I don't get to see her very much since she lives out of town, but I cherished the hugs, the tears, and the memories of Lindsay we shared. Lindsay's friends, Kevin's and my friends, our family, especially little Audrey – they are what keeps me going and what keeps our memories of Lindsay alive.

So, please, keep talking about Lindsay and Inflammatory Breast Cancer. Keep her memory alive and never forget.

FINAL WORDS
March 2, 2020

Lindsay's last post came upon us all unexpectedly, and you may have been left wanting to hear from her one more time. You may find yourself reading back over her posts, realizing how impactful they were, wanting to recall how they made you feel. Her words were that powerful. So, I will leave you with these final words from Lindsay:

My hope is that someday there will be someone that is facing the same battle as me and is feeling as scared as I am, and they come across my posts and realize that they are not alone. My hope is that my transparency, although it may be difficult for my loved ones to read at times, will help someone else someday. Sharing thoughts and experiences creates longevity. No matter what may happen to me, these words and this page will always exist. FYI- I have not lost hope. I am more hopeful than ever and I am at peace. Let me go on record being that girl that says "I'll be the one in a million to beat this."

Videos featuring Lindsay during her journey, and others made in her honor/memory, can be found on my YouTube channel. Search Diane Koster at www.YouTube.com

To learn more about Inflammatory Breast Cancer, or to make a donation in Lindsay's memory, visit **The IBC Network Foundation** (Terry Arnold's organization) at www.theibcnetwork.org, or on Facebook, search IBC Network Foundation.

Proceeds from this book will go into the Lindsay's Legacy Fund, held at the Genesis Health Services Foundation, and will be used to help women in need get the prompt, expert medical attention required to diagnose and treat Inflammatory Breast Cancer.

~

Made in the USA
Monee, IL
25 April 2020